My Life
My Struggle

B.K.Basu Roy Chowdhury

BLUEROSE PUBLISHERS
India | U.K.

Copyright © B.K. Basu Roy Chowdhury 2024

All rights reserved by author. No part of this publication may be reproduced, stored in a retrieval system or transmitted in any form or by any means, electronic, mechanical, photocopying, recording or otherwise, without the prior permission of the author. Although every precaution has been taken to verify the accuracy of the information contained herein, the publisher assumes no responsibility for any errors or omissions. No liability is assumed for damages that may result from the use of information contained within.

BlueRose Publishers takes no responsibility for any damages, losses, or liabilities that may arise from the use or misuse of the information, products, or services provided in this publication.

For permissions requests or inquiries regarding this publication, please contact:

BLUEROSE PUBLISHERS
www.BlueRoseONE.com
info@bluerosepublishers.com
+91 8882 898 898
+4407342408967

ISBN: 978-93-5989-037-1

Cover design: Rishav Rai
Typesetting: Rohit

First Edition: June 2024

This book is dedicated to my wife -Maya, my daughters Jayita, and Ankita, my son in laws, Bhaskar and Indraneil, my grand daughter Anwika, and my grandsons Abhiraj, Ishaan and Ujaan.

Acknowledgements: -

...

I have the usual acknowledgement to make. There are very few of them and even those I must make are only catalytic agents in the production of this memoir. My two daughters, Jayita and Ankita both had evinced keen interest in having a copy, but my elder daughter was constantly monitoring the progress of the book, from time to time, in a sense which worked like a catalytic agent.

To my wife also, I have acknowledgements to make, but none of the usual kind. I have noticed that in the world of book production, most authors advertise a loyal adhesion to their wives. My wife has maintained an objective interest only in the production of this memoir. In our journey of almost forty-two years, she has maintained a calm philosophy of life and has never been excited, by my high faulting moods nor my winged exultations.

On the other hand, she has organized and sustained a balanced regime for me and kept me on an even keel amidst many torments of life. Those who know, what it means in these days to provide a husband with good food and similar amenities of life, and yet how difficult it is for a man to ride on an even keel in the contemporary world will understand my gratitude to wards my wife.

Prologue

...

All of us face challenges in our life. Some face more than their share. How we dare such challenges, shape our future. Our choices, and how we grip them shape the people we turn out to be.

I am eternally grateful that I was born to loving and supportive parents in a country that offered me enormous opportunity and blessings; factors beyond my control that set the stage for my life. Primarily, a family has an enormous impact on a child in its nurturing days. It is generally seen that an Army officer's son generally becomes a defense personnel, a cine actress' daughter follows the footprints of her father. My upbringing was no exception to this. The beautiful nature amidst green forests, deep blue oceanic waves engulfing the Andamans, combined with sudden cyclones, incessant rain almost throughout the year, coupled with a tough life in a semi hilly terrain, and in a cross juncture of the chaotic period of Pre and Post Independence, forced me to harmonize my life with that of nature.

I was the third and youngest child of my parents. My father, a qualified technician in the welding trade, was initially posted at Jabalpur Gun and Shell factory, Madhya Pradesh from where he dared to start life in a completely new place, the Andaman &

Nicobar Islands (popularly known as **Bay Islands**). He was an adventurous man and overcame all challenges of serving in an island which was ravaged and torn apart by the effect of the Second World War. From my schooldays my initial dream was to become a marine engineer, then it was teacher, but destiny forced me to take up engineering profession, as it was my father's wish. Mine was a sort of wild card entry to this profession.

Through this book, I share my journey, my experience both sweet and sour. Life is like an ocean, with innumerable waves involving high tides and low tides. One must learn to sail through life just as a ship navigates through the vastness of the ocean in every kind of weather.

What prompted me to go for this adventure of writing down my memoir?

During our stay in Hyderabad, in March 2020, when the first lockdown was declared due to COVID-19 pandemic, there was no way to overcome the boredom of staying inside the house except, sharing stories of my past life with my granddaughter Doyel and grandson Dron. All my family members listened my life stories with interest and wonder. My daughter, Jayita, alias Dipa, and granddaughter Doyel suggested I should pen down my memoir as it would enable them to preserve it for future reading. With my limited knowledge of English, I have tried my best to portray an honest account of my life, and I trust readers would enjoy the book.

For the convenience of readers, I have broadly divided my biography into four broad sections.

1. Part I- The period from May 1951 till 1977; the period from my birth, childhood and youth, spent in Port Blair, Andaman & Nicobar Islands.
2. Part II- The period from April 1977 (the year I left Port Blair), till October 1995, the year I left Kolkata and moved to IIT-Kharagpur for my fourth job.
3. Part III- The period from 1995 to 31st May 2011, the day I retired from my active service life.
4. Part IV From 2011 till writing of this memoir i.e., 2021.

Contents

...

PART ONE
From 1951-27th April1977 .... *1*

PART TWO
From April 1977 to October 1995) *27*

PART THREE
From 9th October to 31st May 2011 .... *71*

PART FOUR
2011 to 2021 .... *91*

Epilogue 101

PART ONE

From 1951-27th April 1977

...

The impact of the environment coupled with the society in which I grew up, influenced my formative years and continued to shape my career for the years ahead.

Childhood days- Most of the content in these following paragraphs is the verbatim of the stories narrated by my father, when I was very young and loved to hear such stories of wars and heroic deeds. Most of the war stories, especially of World War II, and in particular Japanese occupation in the Andaman &Nicobar Islands, subsequently taken over by British Empire were told by my father, when we assembled for dinner on the dining table which was built by my father himself. My father used to narrate the famous poem of **Casabianca,** and we both sister and brother listened to these stories of valour and courage with awe and rapt silence. Not all readers have heard about the poem. Hence, my brief introduction.

The poem CASABIANCA begins as under: -
"The boy stood on the burning deck,
Whence all but he had fled.

The flame that lit the battle's wreck
Shone round him over the dead"

CASABIANCA is a poem written by poet Felicia Hemans in around 1826. In short, the story depicts the heroic courage of a young boy named **Casabianca,** who stood on the deck of a British ship (which was set on fire by its enemies) and refused to desert his post as ordered by his father, the Master of the ship. Casabianca succumbed to the flames which engulfed his ship.

The poem was written on the backdrop of the famous Battle of the Nile, fought between the French and British navy.

My father used to recite the poem with expression, in a manner that left shivering down my spine. My father said he heard the story from his British boss, Captain Harvey, the Harbour Master of Andaman & Nicobar Islands around 1945.

Wars are universally condemned, but invariably fought. So is the story of World War II, which was fought between 1939 to 1945. The impact of wars are devasting, be it, economic, military, or social. The two great wars of the 20th century were no exception. Having being born in an island, and also experiencing journey through the deep blue sea Bay of Bengal in a big passenger liner, as also short cruise in tug boats, speed boats fitted with a swanky outboard engines, and having gone deep into the engine room of ships, pulled into the dry dock for repairs, all perplexed my mind at a very young age and allowed me to dream that one day I would sail as a Marine Engineer in a merchant navy ship. When I was merely twelve years old, I knew the meaning of the marine technical terms GO AHEAD and ASTERN, BOW and AFT, PORT and the STARBOARD, the meaning of

PROPELLOR, HULL, KEEL, BRIDGE, and such technical terms which are known only to those who are in the business of navigation. The deep blue colour of the sea, it's thundering waves and also the calm and serene look especially on full moon nights, charmed and cherished my memory for many years later.

My early years in Bay Islands

Many of us are born with a silver spoon and have no difficulty in steering through the choppy waves of lives. In many cases, I have seen that affluent parents, by their sheer money power have placed their children in a proper place. On the contrary many of us were born to struggle amidst all odds. Unfortunately, my life has been a struggling one; our family had to virtually fight all the curses of the partition of India, particularly Bengal. Here our family refers to my parents, my elder sister, Rekha,my elder brother Swapan and myself.

I was born and brought up in a frugal Bengali family, a family displaced from East-Bengal immediately after independence in the year 1947. It took one generation to stand up and survive the economic thrust of the partition of India and its aftermath on Bengal. Just as world history is divided into two distinct eras viz; BC and AD, similarly for people residing in the Indian subcontinent, our country is divided into two eras viz; BP (Before Partition) and AP (After Partition). For Bengalis of East Bengal life changed ironically immediately after partition, the woes and sufferings of people were beyond imagination particularly for Bengalis.

This autobiography defines the conditions in which an Indian grew to manhood in the mid of last century, his adventures in the world, where at the end, he is more baffled, and left stranded on such intriguing questions, question as to whether he had breathed a purposeful life? I have tried my best to give a true account of my life which struggled in a hostile environment like the Andaman &Nicobar Islands, from birth till the age of 26 years.

This struggled life of 26years left an idelible mark on my life and helped me in facing all the adversaries of life.

Why an Autobiography?

Men do not become aware of the precise quality of their early years, until late in life. Famous Russian author and autobiographer, Late Sergey Akasov, Rabindranath Tagore, Late Ex President A.P.J. Abdul Kalam, Prof. J.V. Narlikar, the noted astrophysicist, and many eminent people, wrote their autobiographical masterpieces, when they were advanced in age. Whatever the label that I attach to this autobiography, memoir, family history, I have tried to sketch, an honest account of my personal life, without any exaggeration. My life has taught me few lessons, in a harsh way. The fallacy is one has only one life, and whatever needs to be achieved, should be done within this life itself. Some of my hard-earned experiences are:

a) **Patience** –Patience pays in the long run. In my life I have experienced this simple truth time and again. I had to struggle patiently for ten long years to free myself from the bondage of a financial trap, which my father inflicted on me due to his lack of foresight and irresponsible way of spending money, not caring about the future. Finally, I won the battle.

b) **Opportunity-** "A pessimist sees difficulty in every opportunity; an optimist grasps the opportunity in every difficulty"- *said **Winston Churchill.*** In my case too, due to my lack of maturity I missed two golden opportunities to rise in my professional career.

c) "I shall prepare myself, and some day my chance will come"- said **Abraham Lincoln.** This statement holds true for me too. Later in this biography, I shall narrate as to how true this statement is:-

d) **Kindness-** "Kindness is caring for others, even when they may not care for you" I strongly believed and pursued this philosophy in my life whenever I had an opportunity to do so. To a large extent, I am satisfied with this score. My wife at times ridiculed me saying, that friends and acquaintances quite often say "Biman Babu Bhison Bhalo Manush" meaning Mr. Biman is a very kind person. There must be some reason behind them bestowing such an honour, though I never felt elated with such adjectives. I considered that to work for someone is to pray for God.

d) Responsibility -Whenever a responsibility comes on to your shoulder never try to shirk it, we need to remember that it is an order from the God, and therefore do not run away, God is watching you. " You cannot escape the responsibility of tomorrow by evading it to today" said former *American President* **Abraham Lincoln.**

e) Economically downtrodden. Never look down upon a person because he is poor. Today you are rich, tomorrow you may become a pauper. The word **poor** is not by one's choice, it is by one's destiny. I have personally experienced this, as I myself come from a poor family. There is famous poem by Poet Rabindranath Tagore, poem no 108, Gitanjali (a collection of poems), which I would like to narrate here part of it: -

"Jare tumi niche fhalio cho, se to -mare bandhibe je niche,

Paschate rekhecho jare, se tomare paschate taniche."

The meaning of the above two lines are:

"To whom you look down upon, he would tie you at the bottom,"

Those whom you have pushed back, they would drag you from behind."

Today's inspiration and courage to write an auto biography stems from here itself. A lion's share of my energy and enthusiasm in writing this memoir has been drawn from my elder daughter Dipa. From the day she was born, my joy knew no bounds. As I became father and held her passionately between my two arms and thanked God for giving me such a beautiful baby on 6th November 1980 at R. G. Kar Medical College and Hospital, in Shyam Bazar, adjacent to the famous and busiest five point crossing in North Kolkata. Later, I shall narrate how gradually she excelled in all walks of her life and became the most wanted and talked about girl in our society, no matter where she lived, and pursued her studies/career. Thus, these are two pronged catalysts behind my writing this memoir. I am sure, barring a few pages, which at times may be boring, it will be enjoyed by our family members, to whom it is dedicated.

My early life in Andaman and Nicobar(A & N) Islands- My birthplace.

A&N Islands, which is in the Bay of Bengal or 'Kala Pani' *(Black Water)*, has been christened Bay Islands by many authors. It comprises of approximately 572 islands, out of which only 36 are inhabited. The early history of these exquisite, beautiful island is shrouded in mystery. Occupied by East India

Company towards the close of 18th century, they were used by the British empire for a penal settlement after 1857. Prisoners sentenced to life imprisonment were kept in the famous Cellular Jail. The real inhabitants of these islands were however, some aboriginal tribes like Onges, Sentinels, Shompen, Jarwas etc., whose past is mysterious and future uncertain. Today Bay Islands is a popular destination for tourists who love sea.

I was born on 31st May 1951 in G. B. Pant, Govt Hospital, Port Blair, Andaman &Nicobar Islands, as these group of islands lay in Bay Of Bengal. Port Blair is the capital town of Andaman and Nicobar Group of Islands. I have no means of proving this date. My mother, Late Sudha Rani Basu Roy Chowdhury remembered the day to be Wednesday and the time was around 1.45 pm.

We were two brothers and one sister. My elder sister named Rekha, was born on the holy day of 25th of December 1946, birthday of Lord Jesus. Her nickname was Manu. Second to my sister and elder to me, Babu, the recorded name was Swapan(nick name Babu), whose date of birth is precisely not known to me as yet, but was two years elder to me. Both my elder sister and my brother were born with a fair complexion as that of my father, whereas I inherited my mother's complexion which was wheatish. When my elder brother was eight years old and I was six years then, one fine morning, when we were in our neighbour's house, an ambulance carrying my brother's coffin came and stood in front of our house. From the ambulance alighted my mother, my father and my uncle, Kesto Mama, who were there in the hospital through the night by the bedside of my brother, Babu. I faintly recollect, the day when my mother, got down from the ambulance, went straight to our house, embraced both of us and broke down, saying, "I could not bring your brother back home. The news of my brother's death, flashed in our society and people from nearby areas thronged our house. Babu had been suffering from epilepsy, a rare disease for which there was no advanced medical treatment then. He managed his illness well with grace. It was the year 1956, when I was hardly five years old. When my brother was getting frequent fits of epilepsy, two Christian gentlemen, both of them were twin brothers, landed in Port Blair in search of job and both of them got employed. Soon news spread that one of the twin brothers was a gem of palmist. One day my father went to the twin brothers and narrated the illness of my brother. The twin brother wanted to see the right palm of my father and concluded that my brother would not survive his illness, and that within a year he would leave for heaven. My father did not disclose this incident to my mother. Surprisingly my brother left all of us after six months.

I think my mother had known that he would not survive his illness for long. I won't try to describe how deeply we mourn his passing away today. As a fading memory, my mother fondly preserved his school uniform, a nylon (snake like) belt, his tiffin box, and his Khaki school bag, which she caringly carried and preserved in her trunk for the next fifty-two years as a memory, and till she breathed her last in 2008. I wanted to carry on this memory of my late brother, and handover the same to my daughter Dipa, but I failed to do so, because I had to hand over the keys of our single storied house in Barasat to the purchaser in haste, due to local trouble and sensing violence.

My Father's name was Sushil Kumar Basu Roy Chowdhury, a tall, fair complexioned, handsome man. He was a qualified technical staff who was serving the Govt of India's Ordinance factory in Jabalpur in Madhya Pradesh, in 1940, during World

War II. In Hindu religion, a father is revered as equivalent to God. My mother's name was Sudha Rani. I was naturally more drawn towards my mother, when I vividly recall the pain she underwent years after years silently, and the sacrifices she made in bringing up the family. I now feel as to why I had a feeling for my mother. I was born with a soft heart; it was a gift from the God.

Out Break of World War II, and its fall out on the people of Andaman & Nicobar Islands: World War II was fought during the period 1939 -1945. Wars are universally condemned, but invariably fought. Whether the aim is territorial expansion or economic exploitation, they are certainly a cruelty of man over man. The two great wars of the century were no exception to this. The second world war, however had far reaching military, social and economic impact, on the people of Bay Islands and the immense sufferings of the people during the period, forms the core of the history of Andaman & Nicobar Islands. The story of Japanese occupation of Andaman &Nicobar is the central theme in the history of these islands. Today the infamous Cellular jail, where the famous Savarkar brothers were convicted in the Nasik Conspiracy case and was transported to Andamans Islands stands as a monument of historical evidence.

During my father's tenure, in Jabalpur one fine morning the news broke out, asking for technical hands, who are willing to go to Bay Islands for permanent absorption in A&N Islands, GOVT SERVICE, with a 133% hike (Andaman special pay) in the basic pay as DA, free unfurnished quarter, electricity and ration, i.e., essentials food grains etc. My Father got lured and consulted few friends and all likeminded friends and quickly decided to leave Jabalpur for A&N islands to start a fresh and adventurous journey of **KALAPANI**, a Hindi name for black water. The name Kala Pani is not too much out of context. As you set sail from Kolkata port, which is in river Ganges, the color of the water is yellow. As you leave sand head (the confluence of river Ganga and the sea), the color of the sea gradually starts changing.

The next day onwards as you get up and move on to the deck of the ship you find the color of the sea water is light green. As time passes on the light green color changes to blue. On the second day morning you find the water as deep blue and later in the day it is almost black or I would say blue black. and so the name goes as **KALAPANI**

My Father left Jabalpur for his maiden and challenging journey to Andaman &Nicobar Islands in in the year 1945, via Kolkata. I also happen to remember the name of the troop **Ship S.S. Dilwara**, through which he sailed from Kolkata to Port Blair. Prior to leaving Kolkata my father went to East Bengal, where my mother was residing with her in-laws and assured her that he would take her to Port Blair, once everything was settled . On 1st October 1945, my father set sail from Calcutta on board the Ship **S.S. Dilwara**, which was escorted by four other ships. N.K. Paterson, the chief commissioner designates and Brig J.A. Salomon along with British troops around ten thousand were in the Ship. The ship reached Port Blair on 7th October 1945, in the wee hours of 7th October and was anchored off the Ross Islands. Since the present harbor in Chatham Islands, was not big enough and the draught was not sufficient to accommodate such large ship like S.S. Dilwara. The journey of approximately three and half days to four from Kolkata through Kalapani is a frightening experience and a great feeling. If one happens to tour this island, I suggest one should travel by sea. In the year 1946, on 25th December on the auspicious day of Lord Jesus' birthday, my elder sister Rekha was born, in Port Blair, Govt Hospital which was then completely manned by British staff. My elder brother babu was also born in the same hospital in the year 1948 and lastly, I was born on 31st May in 1951.

H.M. Troop ship - S.S.Dilwara

My First Schooling The first schooling is a memorable and cherished event in one's lifetime. I joined my school 'Modern Preparatory School', an English medium co-education school and the only English medium school then at the preparatory level in Port Blair, in Andaman & Nicobar Islands in 1955, when I was about 4 years old. It was being run exactly as per Cambridge Curriculum, with one Bengali Head mistress, Mr Smriti Kana Sanyal, trained in Cambridge System of education in U.K. It had a mixed intake of students coming from all walks of life, we had Burmese, Chinese, Keralites, Tamilians, Coorg and local Andamanese students. Irrespective of caste creed and educational background of parents, these students were given admissions. My elder sister Rekha also studied in the same school.

The school had beautiful objectives. These were learning, and inculcating good manners, as is expected from a Cambridge student. We had a blend of European and Indian teachers. Incidentally the husband of our head mistresses Mihir Kumar Sanyal was a graduate marine engineer from U.K. and was boss of my father. Mrs Sanyal's daughter Gouri was my classmate.

Our school started at 7.30 AM and went up to 12.30 pm. The thrust was more on English speaking and learning, less on academic load, more on manners, etiquettes, dress code and discipline as was expected of a Cambridge students. It was a co – educational school. We had students from all strata of society. The day started with English song followed by National Anthem. I still remember my last day in the school, when we had a picnic inside the school, and we had a lunch along with our teachers and head mistress. I was in the school from 1955 till 1962.

After completing my junior Cambridge education at Modern Preparatory School Port Blair my Head mistress Smt. Sanyal, advised my parents to send me to India for education in a Cambridge convent school, but my parents did not pay much heed as my father had a meagre earning and could not have afforded such expenditure. Consequently, I got admitted to Boy's Higher Secondary Demonstration Multipurpose School, Port Blair. This school was a Hindi medium and under the Central Government. From class 7 to class 11, I had four years of education in this school which was totally free, as a result the background of students, their upbringing, were not commensurate with what I already had. With lot of difficulty, and with the support of my sister, (as she was then the senior most student at the school) helped me in overcoming the initial hurdles of adjusting my academic and co –curricular activities, in a free school vis- a- vis my convent background.

Slowly and steadily, I started moving on to my Hindi medium school and within four years reached Class 11.

I appeared for the Central Board of Secondary Education exam and cleared it with second division marks. I missed the first division mark only by a couple of marks –My score was 58.3%. Given my merit, the hard work, the non- availability of books, teaching and other academic resources, I consider my gradation as reasonable, though at times my family members ridiculed me as a second-class student. I have no regrets as all students are not born intelligent, nor all students are born with a silver spoons. Very early in my career, I knew that my life would be a struggling one, as I came from a humble and frugal family. I started my journey for higher education on a low profile, and wanted to be a teacher, as I respected this profession from the core of my heart. I have a strong conviction that if I had not been taught properly by my teachers in science subjects, I would not have been what I am today. They only prepared me for my journey towards my higher education. During my school days in Govt. Boys school, I had a good number of friends the names of whom I can't miss mentioning here.

a) Yameen Mohd Mustafa, a graduate electrical engineer from Jadavpur University, and now retired as a Superintendent Engineer from Electricity Board of A&N Islands. A sharp Rifle shooter won best shooter award defeating shooters from armed forces in the .303 bore rifle category, when he was mere a student of class-XI.

b) Samshad Ali. He was from Biology stream. A highly skilled crafts man, who taught me how to ride a scooter, could open the lock of any scooter or bike. A true friend from the core of my heart.

c) Rohinder Lal Shah. Poularly known as Rohin. Rohin's father was our school headmaster. Rohin's mother was a kind lady and had a deep affection for me. Whenever I visited his home, I used to to have lunch in their house. I had a deep respect for her. Rohin did his M.S. from AIIMS, New_Delhi and has his own eye hospital in Port Blair.

Till today, after fifty years of separation, they still continue maintaining friendly relations.

After leaving the corridors of my school life in Port Blair, in 1968 I was not sure about my future plan, but I had a passion for Physics and wanted to become a teacher in physics. I left Port Blair and came to Calcutta for admission in any college under Calcutta University (CU), but my luck was so bad that throughout the length and breadth of the city of Calcutta, I could not secure a honors seat in physics in any college under CU .We then went to Kalyani University, where the HOD (physics) gave some hope seeing my marks. But since admission was already in progress, he could not assure me of anything. We returned to Kolkata and waited for a response from Andaman &Nicobar administration for a reserved seat in any engineering college in India. Interview letter came from Kalyani University, asking me to report for admission in B.Sc. (Honors) course in physics. I was glad, my mother too was. But my father was not at all happy. With in next three days, there was a telegram from A&N administration asking me to report before the Registrar, Annamalai University, Chidambaram, Tamil Nadu, for a seat in Mechanical Engineering. My father was very keen to send me to study engineering. After few rounds of discussions among family members, it was decided that we shall proceed to Annamalai

University, which was by the side of Chidambaram Station, Tamil Nadu.

As we boarded the taxi for Howrah station, I saw tears rolling down from my mother's cheek. This is the first time after the death of my elder brother Swapan alias Babu, I saw my mother weeping. I was in a sad mood. Any way after two days of night journey, through Madras mail we reached Madras, from where we boarded another train from **Egmore** station and around 1.30 pm we reached Chidambaram station,.We de-boarded the train at Chidambaram station and moved into a small lodge. Took bath, lunch, and took rest for the day. My father's excitement was at it's top.

Next day we took a bullock cart and went to Annamalai University, Administrative building and met the Registrar. The Registrar informed us that there are many students from Andaman and Nicobar Island as well as Bengali students from Agartala, Tripura. After completing the formalities, we came back and met the dean of the Dept of Engineering and Technology, paid fees and finally got enrolled for a 5yr integrated course in Mech. Engineering. Thus, my journey to become an engineer began from Annamalai University in the year 1968.

My father requested all students from the Andamans that my son is late in his admission and to help him in overcoming his academic shortcomings. My father was entertained for two days in the hostel guest room and after enquiring from me about my college and course, decided to leave for Kolkata.

All the senior students went to Chidambaram station to see off my father, with an assurance that they would look after me. Thus, my dream of becoming a Physics Professor ended and I began attending classes of first year engineering.

At the tender age of 17years, I had to face the ordeal of the following pain for a period of three months:

a) The pain of separation from home, parents and school friends, thousands of kilometers away.

b) The mental trauma of ragging. At times I used to weep asking God where you have sent me? How long this ordeal shall continue?

c) Late joining and its cascading effect on academics, and not being able to grasp subjects like Calculus Analytic geometry and Engineering drawing added to my trauma.

In such a tormented situation god sent a Samaritan student, named shri Ajit Kumar Nandi, a final year student of Mech. engineering stream, who assured my father at Chidambaram station that your son will have no problem. It happened in true sense.

Shri Ajit Kumar Nandi was the class representative for final year Mechanical stream, very good in studies, a very good football player and everyone loved him for his amicable manners. He had a good rapport with all teaching and non-teaching staff, mess staff and others.

I told him Ajit Da, "I am not following Calculus, Co-ordinate geometry and Engineering Drawing. Next, he took me to a lecturer in Math who agreed to guide me in understanding the basics of Calculus. One hour of lecture in his room helped me in catching up with the basic concepts of Limits and differential calculus. He also engaged another Sr. student of Third year who exposed me to Co-ordinate geometry. For the drawing part, he talked with the Lecturer and in the drawing class itself, he took extra care to see that I had no problem in understanding geometrical drawing. My seniors from the Andamans provided me with books, drawing instruments, and other academic resources.

At Annamalai University, Department of Engineering, I had a couple of Seniors from Andamans. I shall be failing in my task if I do not mention the names of a few of my closest friends with whom I shared my memorable days in Annamalai University and beyond.

a) Shri. Jageshwar Singh - A third year student from Civil Engineering stream. A very good hockey player of Annamalai University, with whom I spent my holiday period while the college went on student strike. We spent almost a month in Madras City, staying in a cheap hotel roaming around the city in the daytime and watching movies during the nighttime. Shri Singh also blatantly saved me from the turmoil of ragging by his classmates, when it was known that I too belonged to Port Blair. Shri Singh retired as S.E. from Andaman PWD and is settled in Port-Blair.

b) The Second name which comes to my mind is that of shri Manohar Singh. He was four years senior to me in college and was from Mechanical Stream. When I joined Port Blair Electricity Dept. in 1973, he was my boss and helped me understand several engineering intricacies of a diesel as well as steam power plant. He was a brilliant student in our college. Both in electrical and mechanical engineering stream he had tremendous grip.

c) The other two students were Late Krishneswar Lal, and late S.V. Krishna. Shri Krishneswar Lal left us for his heavenly abode while he returned from his educational tour in his fourth year and got infected with Hepatitis, and was treated at Madras Medical college, but did not survive. Shri S.V. Krishna died in an accident while serving Electricity Department, Port-Blair. My humble and respectful tributes to both of them. May their souls rest in peace.

Coming back to Annamalai university, Gradually, I started making friends with first year students and settled down. I also wrote letters to my father about my life at the university and the help I got from seniors from Tripura and the Andamans. My father wrote me back that, I should concentrate on my studies, keep contact, and pay respect to the seniors, like Ajit Da(From Tripura) and Shri Raghunandan Singh (from Port Blair).

There was a gulf of difference in my method of learning during my school days and that of Annamalai University style. Here in the University no one carried any books, and everyone depended upon the lecture notes given by the subject-teachers. I had many doubts, which I could not clear myself as I did not have any textbook with me. In the true sense also, there were no textbooks written or available which was attuned to the syllabus of Annamalai University.

My college teachers

Among so many teachers who taught us various subjects, right from first year to final year, none could inspire me or come close to my heart except two teachers, the name of whom I ought to mention, as my deep respect towards them.

The first teacher was math's lecturer shri D. Rama Ratnam. The most beautiful trait was his wit, style and movement, practically dancing from one end of the rostrum to the other end.

He could paralyze students into immobile silence the whole crowd of turbulent freshers, at a glance of his eyes.

To make us learn the concept of differential calculus, for three months at a stretch only taught us the concept of **Limits** and what happens when Limit Δ tends to ∞. I was amazed to see the speed with which he used to solve problems. From Shri Rama Ratnam only I got a natural affinity for Calculus, even today Calculus remains as my most amazing subject in mathematics. In second year, he taught us how to calculate the areas of geometrical figures by using **Integral calculus.**

Till the second year the academic journey was smooth. All academic chaos started from third year onwards. Subjects like **Strength of Materials, Thermodynamics and Theory of machines**, appeared like wild beasts that slithered their way into the lives of average students of third year mechanical engg batch to which I was no exception. None of the subject teachers could instill a sense of confidence among average students like us.

For the first six months we grappled and did not know how to overpower these three beasts, and it continued till final exams.

As regards **strength of materials**, we had some exposure in the second year, hence it was not that too difficult. In between there was a strike, and I sailed to Port-Blair with a good book from our library. During the period of the strike, which was one month, I worked hard to understand the basics of **strength of materials** i.e., Bending Moment Diagrams and the Shear Force Diagrams and was able to solve problems of my own. For the whole year I had the textbook with me and strictly followed our teacher, who was following the syllabus. As time rolled by, I was confident of clearing the subject. As far as **Theory of machines** was concerned, there was no way out, and I decided to meet with my fait accompli. But I was very regular in attending my classes, to fetch good marks on attendance. At times the HOD, who used to take the classes used to hand over the class to a fresh lecturer, due to his pre-occupation. This fresh lecturer by name Iyenkaran was a brilliant guy, and had a strong grip on the subject, when students virtually gheraoed him, whenever there was a was a chance, and cleared all their doubts. Good students used to help average students like me, whenever there was such an academic crisis. This also helped me to a large extent. Later, I felt that this subject is highly teacher oriented.

As the days of exam approached, at least 80 %of the students were left disappointed. In the meantime, I gathered a lot of courage to meet. Prof V. Muthhuverrapan, as my seniors told me he was a very good teacher and an M.S. From Cornell University, USA. Prof Muthhuverrapan was a highly academic person who understood my problem, gave me a printed copy of the syllabus, last three years question papers and recommended an ELBS cheap textbook, which was there in the library. Even today after approx. fifty years, I remember the name of the ELBS book "Engineering Thermodynamics" by Y R Mathew. Without uttering a word, I coolly walked out of his room and did not mention anything to any of my students or roommates. The academic classes were suspended for practical and study leave.

Without wasting a single day, I started revising the subject as per the syllabus and textbook provided. Over the passage of time, within three weeks I started holding a grasp of the subject, and before the exam I was confident that I would clear the subject. At the same time, curiously enough, I had a liking for the subject. Even today I have a liking for the subject and understand the importance of the subject. The following are my scores in the third-year final exams: -

- Strength of Materials-69/130, (pass mark being 52)
- Theory of Machines-52/130, (just cleared.).
- Thermodynamics-57/130. -(Pass mark is 52)

From the above marks, one can gauge how precarious was the situation? After the results were declared my friends asked Basu! How did you clear these three subjects?,I told them, it was God's grace. I cleared the final exam in one go. Lot of my friends failed and cleared in the supplementary exams, which were held in September each year.

Next two years was a smooth journey, and I appeared for the final exam. I cleared the final exam in one go. Even today I considered myself lucky that I got the class which I deserved i.e., second class. But I have no regrets.

After graduation from Mech. Engineering from Annamalai University in 1973, I had no other option but to revert to Port Blair. Incidentally, in the same year, my elder sister tied her knot with Dr. Barid Kanti Ray, an Associate Professor in Physics at IIT Kharagpur. After completing the marriage rituals, we sailed back to Port Blair with a heavy heart. My father was a bit upset, as he had a very soft corner for her as is normal.

As usual my mother was happy that she could find a son –in-law after years of waiting. On the contrary my father was in a pensive mood as he had to part with his only daughter and first child, nick named 'Manu'. After three days of sailing in high seas, through Bay of Bengal, we reached port Blair in July 1973. After reaching Port Blair I was desperately looking forward to my final year results from my first-year college mate, Shri Jayaprakasam.

Luck favored me, and I received a telegram that I along with my friend Jayaprakasam, cleared the final exam in one go. My father, in his sheer joy, wrote letters to all our relatives about my results. After a fortnight I, received my mark Sheet and a provisional certificate. But then came the real challenge, as the Govt of A & N Islands, relieved me from my three years bond., as there was no job in the islands.

Not knowing exactly what to do next, after graduation, because those days getting a job was a herculean task, as there was surplus of engineers, unlike these days when jobs are provided through college placements. With in next few days, one of our acquaintances came and informed us that the Govt. Electricity Dept, of A&N island was in need of Junior Engineers. Without losing time I applied, cleared interview and was given appointment as Junior Engineer, and was placed in a scale of Rs425-700/-. Every one of us in our family heaved a sigh of relief. My first home take salary was around Rs 700/-which on receipt, handed over to my mom, who got emotional as I handed over the cash to her. After my sister's marriage, (who had funded my engineering scholarship), there was a dip in the financial income, which again bounced back after few months. My mother thanked Goddess Lakshmi for her kind blessings.

5th September1973 was a memorable day in my life and my professional carrier. On this day I joined my first service as a Junior Engineer in the Govt, Electricity Department Port Blair. [For 38 years since 1973, I was employed and finally laid down my office on 31st May,2011]. During these 38 years of my career, I have learnt many lessons, some of which I shall share with you all. When I look back, I find that my father's decision to go for a professional career was justified, as I fully enjoyed my career as a professional mechanical engineer.

The four years (1973-1977) of my service with the Govt Electricity Dept was a rich experience which I gathered as a junior engineer, especially with operation and maintenance of Diesel Generating sets of various capacities and make. Not only that, but I also had to learn many things about electrical engineering too, as it was a power station.

The beauty of working in a power plant is that a Mech. engineer must learn electrical, and an electrical engineer must learn Mech. engineering. After four years of training cum learning as Junior Engineer, doing shift duty in thermal plants, both coal and diesel, I appeared for an interview before UPSC for a post of Asst. Engineer, Junior Class I (gazette post), in the scale s 700-1300/- considered to be a meteoric rise in those days in Govt. Service. The post was for maintenance of fishing trawlers under Exploratory Fisheries Project, under Ministry of Agriculture, Govt. of India. It is important to mention here that the lion's share of maintenance of a fishing trawler is the maintenance of its powerhouse which is invariably a diesel engine in the engine room. Among the candidates present on the interview board I was the youngest. I remember few questions the board members asked were -

a) By seeing the colour of the exhaust gas, how will you conclude that your Diesel engine is in good working condition??

b) What is the normal temperature range inside a cylinder of a diesel engine.??

c) How does a pyrometer work?

I answered all the question with ease and confidence, the reason being, for every doubt I had during my days as **junior engineer** I used to ask my seniors in the department as well as Sr. engineers (who were deputed by the Central Govt, to Port Blair under the aegis of Central Electricity Authority. Under Ministry of Power) and I also used to refer my books, whenever I had doubts.

I may confidently say that my college days training in my father's Marine dockyard workshop coupled with the extensive training as junior Engineer in the Electricity dept (diesel power station) helped me in improving my technical knowledge to a large extent and put me on an even keel as a mechanical engineer.

I wasn't sure about my performance till I received a telegram from UPSC (UNION PUBLIC SERVICE COMMISSION), confirming my selection.

I received the final appointment -cum posting letter. I was posted at Kandla Port station, under Dist. Kutch, Gandhidham, Gujarat. At this juncture I was in a dilemma whether to join or not as the post against which I had applied was meant for Port-Blair and that I was in no mood to leave Port-Blair.

Many of our acquaintances, who had come to Port Blair directly from Central Govt Services, on hearing the news advised me not to forgo the job, but because of my love for my mother land I was not very keen to leave Port Blair. I could feel the inner desire especially, for my mother who had come to a remote island, immediately after her marriage and spent 32 years (from 1946 - 1977), toiling hard to raise a family of three children, out of which, she lost her son, but because there was no proper treatment, that could be meted out to him, because of staying in a remote Islands like Andaman &Nicobar Islands. Life was very tough on these islands right from food, drinking water, education etc. One beauty of my mother was she used to speak less but her body language was such that you could read it very easily, her likes and dislikes. Lastly, after a lot of discussions I gave in. In the meantime, my father retired in 1975, making me the sole breadearner of the family.

Thus, we started to pack off and out of Port Blair with lock stock and barrel and decided to bid-adieu to Andaman and Nicobar Islands. While in Port Blair I had a clear road map of my career path; from Junior Engineer to Asst. Engineer to Ex. Engineer to Superintendent (Supt) Engineer. There was no post beyond Supt. engineer, thus it was reasonable for me to expect and aspire for this position, but then with the acceptance of the post of Asst. Engineer in Exploratory Fisheries Project, I was sailing through an unchartered sea. Anyway, in the meantime around 1st week of April I was offered an appointment letter by the Ministry of Agriculture &Irrigation directing me to report before The Director Exploratory Fisheries project, P.O. Kandla Port, Dist., Kutch, Gandhidham, Gujarat. In the year 1975, we purchased a piece of land around seven Katah (around5000 sq feet), in Saroj-Park, P.O., Dist., Barasat. West-Bengal.Though I was not keen to purchase such a big piece of land ,but my father's argument was three and half Katah will be utilized for making a house with garage and the balance will be used for gardening which was a hobby for my father since his childhood and indeed he was very passionate about it .I did not resign from the post of Junior Engineer in Electricity dept but requested the administration to permit me to proceed on lien, so that in case I wish, I can revert back to my parent organization; ie,Govt. Electricity Dept. Port Blair.

A farewell was organized by my Dept, on the last day of my office and I was so emotional that my voice got choked and hardly, I could not speak anything. I came back home. My father summoned my Choto mama (UNCLE), who was in Car-Nicobar Islands, and help us in packing our furniture, which was a laborious job, as in those day professional packers were not available. Next few days were spent on meeting friends and well-wishers..

PART TWO

From April 1977 to October 1995)

...

Next day morning our ship M.V. Andamans was to sail at 11a.m. and we boarded around 8am. Many of our friends and acquaintances came to the sailing harbour to see us off. At 11 a.m. there was a warning siren, asking all the visitors to leave the ship and go ashore, the gangway was removed, and our ship gradually tugged off from the harbor, and started taking its cruise. We waived from the waiving gallery of our ship and bid farewell to my mother land leaving our friends and relatives behind. Myself, my father, and my mother all stood on the deck of the ship. We set sail for four days on the choppy seas of Bay of Bengal. After south China sea, it is said that sea of Bay of Bengal is the second most deadly ocean among the various oceans around the globe. After three and half days of rolling and tossing over Bay of Bengal we reached Kolkata Kidder pore Docks (Now Named as Netaji Subhas Dock) where we were allowed to disembark. We got down at around 7.30pm in the evening but could not leave the dock as our luggage remained in the cargo hold of the ship. At 10.30 pm in the dark, when all the passengers left, I went out of the dock to fetch a truck, negotiated the rates and left for Barasat. We reached

Barasat, our aunt's house at around 12.30 a.m., tired and exhausted had our dinner and went to bed.

From the next day, my Mesho and my father went out in search of a rented house whereas I went to Esplanade for booking my ticket for my onward journey from Howrah to Gandhi Dham en route Ahmedabad. A house on rent was located and my father, Mesho and I together shifted and checked in the rented house. The next day, I, along with my father and my uncle (Mesho) and my Baro Mama came to Howrah station. I boarded Ahmedabad express for the first leg of journey. The train left at 8.30 p.m., and I slipped into my first-class coup, which was non-AC and had four sleeper berths only. The only thing my father told me was that I should not forget to send a telegram once I reach my duty station i.e., Kandla.

I must acknowledge here that my father had great confidence in my ability after I graduated and specially after I was selected for the post of Asst Engineer in the Exploratory Fisheries project., and wanted me to be a strong man, both physically and mentally. I strongly believe that it is a natural aspiration of almost all parents that they would like to see their children prosper, and my father was no exception to it. My father joined the services of the Andaman &Nicobar administration as a technician in 1945 and retired as a Chargeman. As the train moved off of the platform I went back to my seat and was churning my memoirs of life at port Blair. Still, I was not sure whether the decision to quit Port Blair was a wise decision or not. But I had my own level of confidence that wherever I might be, I would work, honestly and with dedication, with a focus on my career and should not belie the expectations of my parents or my boss. I wanted them to be proud parents and I did not want my mother to work anymore as a labor.

Now I had to take the baton from them, let them relax and enjoy what they missed during their thirty years, toiling with hard work and labor just to see that their children became worthy of being good citizens.

My mother prepared some paratha and cooked vegetables after consuming which I, rolled on to my bed for the day. Next day morning we crossed Rourkela, the steel town ship in Orissa and in the evening, we reached Nagpur at around 6.30 p.m. At Nagpur I got off the train, bought some oranges and finished my dinner with hot puri and bhaji. There was a change of engine and the train halted for about 20 minutes. Next day around 4pm, I got off at Ahmedabad railway station, went to the enquiry and enquired about the next available train to Gandhidham. I was told that the next train to Gandhidham was around 11pm in the night. had a first-class ticket paper ticket right from Howrah to Gandhidham.

I deposited my luggage in the cloak room, had a cup of tea and went to the retiring room for rest. At around 8.30 pm, I came out and booked a coolie and enquired about the next train to Gandhidham and asked him to come to the retiring room to wake me up, should I fall asleep. I took my dinner at the Ahmedabad Railway station base kitchen, which in those days was really good, and went back to my rest room. As usual the porter came, and we slowly moved to the platform exact. The porter told me the train was an express train from Bombay to Gandhidham. We stood in front of the first-class coach. Truly speaking, I did not have much idea of rail travel and was under the impression that since I had a first-class ticket, I am eligible to board any train. The concept of reservation was not very clear to me.

The train Bombay Gandhidham Express was at the right time. and entered the platform, I checked in the first-class coach, found one berth vacant and occupied the same. With in few minutes came another gentleman and asked me to vacate the seat., as he had a confirmed first-class ticket from Ahmedabad to Gandhidham. I was in no mood to vacate the seat. This gentleman asked me to show my ticket. To this I got furious, and asked him as to who the hell he is to ask my ticket? He started threatening me saying, he would call the TTE (Travelling Ticket Examiner). I said hell with your TTE. Call any damn person! I care to hoots. Getting nervous he went out and called the TTE. The TTE came in and asked me to show my ticket. On seeing my ticket, the TTE politely told me, that though I have a first-class ticket, since I did not have onward reservation, from Ahmedabad to Gandhidham, I cannot travel through this first-class coach. The TTE told the fellow passenger that I had a first-class ticket, and therefore I am as important as he was, as far as railways are concerned. In this dilemma and hot exchange of words, the train blew the whistle and started rolling out. Since I was having full luggage of bedding trunk, suitcase, bucket and what not. The TTE helped me quickly in disembarking the train. I jumped off the running train collecting my luggage and sat over them, remembering my school days poem, JOHNY HEAD IN AIR, by Heinrich Hoffman.

"Do not despair,

For Johny head in air.

He sleeps as sound,

As Johnny underground"

Seeing my condition on the platform, the same porter came close to me and asked Sir! what happened? After hearing my melodrama, he said the next train was a passenger train at around

1.30 pm, and that I shall have no problem in boarding the train., as it was a passenger train and would be almost empty. The temperature in Ahmedabad in those days were unbearable.

Summer was at its at its peak in Ahmedabad and I (being a first-class passenger) was lying on the platform lying on my bed holder almost past midnight and was damn tired and feeling sleepy Any way life must move on so for me too, and I was no exception.

Around 2 a.m. the passenger train arrived, and the porter helped me board the train with my luggage., The train was half empty, and I laid down unfolding my bed holder, on a second class 3tier berth. The coolie seeing me in worn out condition assured me that this train would ultimately take me to Gandhi Dham. He also told me that I would reach Gandhi Dham the next day evening. The attendance in the compartment was very thin. Having been assured by the porter, I de-coupled my bedding, took out pillows and lied down not knowing what trauma was waiting for me in the next few hours. Gradually the train started moving and I thanked my God "Thakur Rama Krishna" I said to God "Che sera, sera"

At around 6.30 am the next morning I got up and found the compartment was totally empty. The tea vendors were shouting "Chai Chai". Passengers on the platform were brushing their teeth. I could sense something has gone wrong. I called a coolie and asked him," What is this station? he replied. "This is Viramgam" I asked him if this train will go to Gandhidham? he replied, "No this bogie will be cut off, you should immediately get down and go to the next bogie". I saw the rail signal; it was already yellow. I immediately called the porter for his help. He came in, took out my luggage and within seconds we boarded the next coach and the train started moving. In a hurry burry I paid him some money and boarded the train. By sheer God 's grace I could avail the train for Gandhidham. After an hour or so the TTE came and asked for my ticket. When I showed him the ticket, he started stared at me, and after hearing my ordeal, was very sympathetic and arranged a berth for me in two tier sleeper coach. I asked him whether the same coach would take me to Gandhidham, to which he said yes.! I remember the old adage, once bitten twice shy. I relaxed and climbed the two-tier berth and went for rest, as the previous night drama ended there, and I was relaxed.

In those days, I mean around 1977, there was no system of carrying drinking water while in train, and almost every passenger used to get down at the station and quenched their thirst from public drinking water kiosk. As the train's steam engine roared and gushed through the semi-arid zone of Gujarat, I was lying and wondering, where am I going? At around noon I was feeling hungry and got down from my berth and occupied a window seat and waited for the station to arrive. As soon as the train stopped against a signal, some vendors approached for water. It was scorching heat and summer was at its peak. Two full earthen pot glass of water costed me Rs1/-, I was hungry too and took some puri bhaji filled my stomach and again went to my berth for a sleep. I was half awake thinking whether my decision to join the post was a correct one, because, I cannot go back and I have to face my luck –fait accompli. At around 4pm, my train entered Gandhidham station and end was my journey. I reached my destination station for my second job.

My condition was such of a defeated soldier returning to his camp as an unsung hero. As I alighted from my train, worn and torn with my bag and baggage, along with a porter and was coming out of **Gandhidham** station, a person with a chauffer's dress approached me and asked, "Kider jane ka Saab? in a typical kachhi (native of Rajasthan) accent, where do you want to go, Sir. I did not pay any heed next time he asked. Saab fishery office me jane ka??then I stopped and asked him," who are u, and how did you come to know that I intend to go to fisheries department"?

He said "Sir. In the morning there was a train, I could not find you, my Saab told me that, in the evening there was another train, and that You may come". True I gave a telegram before leaving Kolkata, about my expected date of arrival, and to arrange for vehicle and accommodation.

Any way he took charge of my luggage, and took me to a hotel for refreshment, after taking a masala dosa and mango juice he took me to the Kandla Port Trust official guest house, where my accommodation was booked for the next three days, dropped me there and left for his home, with an assurance to come the next day for my visit to Kandla Fisheries Project Office, at Kandla Port., where our office was located. After three nights of travel with such nightmare experiences, I was exhausted, took a bath and lied down. Meanwhile the attendant from Kandla guest house got a cup of tea and enquired about my menu for dinner, apprised me of the dinner timings and left. I took tea and again lied down. The next day morning I was ready after my breakfast, and drove around 20 kms and reached our office. The head of office, Dy Director was on leave and Therefore Mr. Sule the Head Clerk (Bara Babu), Mr. Rao, accountant and my workshop staff all were ready for my reception at the entrance to my office. Mr. Sule introduced all the office staff and the workshop staff, and directed me to my office, which was typical of a central government office. It was 27th April 1977, I still remember the date. Immediately, I sent a telegram to my father informing me about my safe arrival and that I had joined my office. Since it was an off season for the fishing trawlers to venture into the sea, both the trawlers were anchored at the jetty which was another five minutes' walk from my office.

Two trawlers, one M.V. Meena Udyog and the other M.V. Kalyani (M.V. stands for Motor vessel, which means it is driven by diesel engine, unlike S.S. which means it is steam ship and driven by steam engine) were there in the jetty. On hearing my arrival, the two skippers came to meet me and wanted to know, whether I was keen to see the vessels. I told them, that I would like to see both the vessels the next day. Again Mr. Sule the Office Superintendent, enquired about my meal and said he would arrange from the canteen of Kandla Port and after lunch he would take me to a Bengali gentleman Mr. Bhattacharyya, who was then Superintendent of a very big office in Kandla Port trust. After getting myself introduced to Mr. Bhattacharya who invited me to his house. Mr.Bhattacharya arranged for my accommodation and food through his strong network of Bengali families in Kandla Port within three days. Thus, I took a small room of an apartment as monthly rent, and for my food I had to walk down to Mr. Chakraborty's residence for morning breakfast and evening tea and two square meals for Rs 150/-.Gradually I settled down. The next day I visited my base workshop, and the two trawlers, observing that one of the two trawlers was in good condition. I mean it was seaworthy, whereas the other one had serious problems in its prime mover i.e., Engine. As such there was no workload at all in my office. Within a week's time my boss joined, and we had a detailed discussion on all aspects of our base activities. Our Deputy Director, Dr. Sulochanan advised me to visit the Chief engineer Mr. Palsane of Kandla Port Trust, to explore the availability of their Dry Dock for annual survey and dry-docking repairs. Mr. Palsane the Chief Engineer regretted that they will not be able to spare their floating dry Dock as their vessels are in queue and it will take about two months to clear the back log of waiting vessels of KPT itself. Thus, I had to return empty handed and inform my boss Dr. Sulochanan.

Since my childhood, I had very fair idea of ship repair, because my father worked in Govt. Marine Dockyard or Shipyard, which was the only one in Andaman & Nicobar Islands built by Britishers. But I did not have any idea of a floating dry dock which I, saw for the first time in Kandla Port, which is in Arabian sea. The sea is very rough from the month of May onwards, and the vessel cannot go out for fishing, and is the time for annual survey and dry-docking repairs. My Boss Dr. Sulochanan, called for a meeting along with the skippers of the two vessels and wanted to know as to when they can leave for Mazagon Dock, Bombay for Annual survey and dry-docking repairs. Around the third week of May 1977, the two vessels left for Bombay, and I left about a week later from my station i.e.; Gandhidham to Bombay. Another thrilling experience was waiting for me as I was new to Bombay, I was not worried about my lodging expenditure or food, but my worry was to complete my assignment of getting the two vessels repaired and come back to my station Kandla. This was a great responsibility, with no one to guide me and was a testing time for me. On the other hand, I was too keen to see the city, and experience its joy and fun.

After three days since the vessels sailed for Bombay from Kandla Port, I started my train journey from Gandhidham to Bombay Central. Someone on the train guided me to get down at Bombay Central and go to the other side of the platform and board the train for Andheri, to reach my Guest house. In the wee hours of the day, I got off at Andheri Station, and was amazed to see the speed of the local trains. Within half an hour I was at the CIFE (Central Institute of Fisheries Education Bombay guest house at Saat (7) Bungalow, Andheri. Since I had sent a telegram intimating my arrival, Guest house boy welcomed me and allotted a room, showed me the bell switch for any assistance. I went to my room, changed my dress and lied down. At 7a.m. I got up and pressed the bell and asked for a cup of tea. As soon as the tea was served, the guest house boy wanted to know my breakfast menu and told me about the timings. As I came to the dining table the guest house boy informed me that CIFE, Director, who was residing in the nearby campus, wanted to meet me. After finishing my breakfast, I went to his residence and introduced myself. After a brief exchange of pleasantries, he wanted to know the purpose of my journey. As the discussion progressed, I came to understand that the Director's post in my Office i.e.; Exploratory fisheries project was vacant and currently Director CIFE is looking after the Directorship of our office too. After half an hour of discussion I left his residence. Of course, he directed me to go to the office of the Dy. Director of EFP (Exploratory fisheries project) at Colaba Fisheries harbour. From Andheri station I reached Church Gate, the terminating station. For the first time, I saw Church Gate station. As I Alighted from the Church Gate station, I came to the bus stop enquired about the bus and stood in the que. As the bus for Colaba approached, passengers started boarding the bus and when all the seats were filled up, and the bus was about to ply, I jumped and got into the bus. Seeing my arrogance, the conductor stopped the bus and asked me to get off the bus. I asked him the reason! He started replying to me in Marathi, and I told him to speak in English. All the passengers were surprised at my arrogance and stupidity. The conductor told me in Hindi to get off the bus and asked me to come in the next bus. I immediately understood my folly and got off the bus. Within in few minutes next bus was there, and I got into it and within half an hour I got down at the last stop, which was the terminal stop. It was very hot and dry in Bombay. As I entered the office, enquired about the office of the Dy. Director and went upstairs. Dr. Radha Krishnan was there in his office. I entered his office and introduced myself. He was very happy to see me, welcomed me and assured me of all help and support. I heaved a sigh of relief. Since the Asst engineer of Bombay station had already resigned and was under the notice period, Dr. Radhakrishnan requested me to help him in engineering matters to which I readily agreed. He advised me to go to the EFP project head office at Phiroj Shah Mehta Road, Botwala chambers Bombay and meet my technical head Ex. Engg Mr. Bhaduri.

Mr. Bhaduri was a Bengali gentle man as his name suggest and was in the EFP, since its inception and had wide experience in repair and maintenance of fishing trawlers. Radhakrishnan gave a free hand to use his official jeep, as he seldom used the jeep. I took the jeep and went to his office and met him. He was a kind gentle man and was happy to meet me. He briefed me about my priorities, and I left his office and came back to Kolaba i.e., Bombay station office. It is important to note here that the EFP had its base station almost on all ports starting from Kandla and ending with Port Blair. After reaching I found the Asst Engineer, Mr. Rao. in his Chamber and he welcomed me to Bombay. He gave me all nitty grits of the Bombay Base station, and the scope of the duties and responsibilities of Asst Engineers in the Bombay office, I came to know that he had a lucrative offer from M/S Union Carbide, which had then imported two fishing trawlers from Poland and was making a roaring business in catching shrimps and lobsters and were exporting them. I requested him to help me in repair of my vessels at Mazagon Dock Bombay, as I was too new to the city. Mr. Rao readily agreed as he had another one month to get himself relieved from the post. Mr. Rao was very kind to me and offered to take me to the Mercantile Marine Department (MMD) a body under the Shipping and Transport Ministry Controlling and regulating all affairs of the shipping Industry. Mr. Rao took me and introduced me to a ship surveyor who was normally assigned by the Principal Surveyor (PS) under the Bombay region to undertake the survey of fishing trawlers. Mr. Rao also told me that at any rate I should first meet the principal survey (P.S) and then, he would assign the task to some surveyor of his choice. The next day, I dressed up neatly and took a blue diary and a blue pen and went to the Office of the Principal Survey (PS) opposite Bombay's Church Gate railway station. At around 10.30am I reached his office, and his secretary asked me to fill the visitors slip and wait for my turn. I was amazed to see that all guest were around 45-50 yrs. of age, and were in suit, boot and tie. I was under the impression that I may not get a chance to meet him. The fever of nervousness crept in me, and I was looking for washroom, when the personal secretary asked me inside. It was a big room with grand furniture and the gentle man was an aged person with broad face and high-powered glasses. His Appearance was that of a fiercely tiger, about to pounce upon me. Abruptly he asked me to take my seat. After knowing my educational background and experience, he was amazed to note that I came from Andaman &Nicobar Islands, he took much interest in me, and started ragging me, and forced me to surrender before him and accept that I was a big zero as far as repair of sea going vessels were concerned.

The first question he asked me was about the length of my fishing trawlers. Smartly I replied around 100 meters. On the very first question he floored me, and he said, was I joking. He told me Mr. Biman Kumar Basu, the Indian trawlers are not more than 50 meters long. Actually, later I found that one trawler was 17 meters and the other was 20 meters. He asked me how many trawlers I wanted to take into dry dock. I answered, Sir one trawler only. He asked me first dry dock my vessel and then, come back to him. He shall assign me a surveyor. As I wanted to leave his room, he advised me saying "Mr. Basu, roaming with blue pen and diary, will not work. You have to work hard." before saying goodbye I assured him," Sir, I shall try my best to follow your advice". As I left his room, I was feeling very dejected and asked myself, "Oh!! Lord where have you dumped me?" But I was not to be cowed down. For learning any aspect of my profession, I can go to any extremes. Technically I got a poor rating by the P.S. Anyway, **tempus fugit.** The next job was to meet the officials of Mazagon Dock, to get a berth for my vessel in any of their Drydocks. Quickly, I went back to Colaba Station to know if the vehicle was required by any other official, because there was only one vehicle allotted to the Colaba fishing station. After releasing the vehicle, I went for lunch, finished my lunch and came back to my office and apprised Dr. Radhakrishnan of the days proceeding. Dr Radhakrishnan was kind enough to enquire about my lunch and advised me to release the vehicle, as he needed the vehicle to meet the Officiating Director. In the second half I met the Skippers of the two trawlers and apprised them of the progress in getting the surveyor and the dry dock. Each day was precious for me, and without any one's help, I had to carry out all the responsibilities myself. Anyway, way next day morning I quickly reached office and asked the vehicle from Dr. Radha Krishnan.

Dr. Radhakrishnan was indeed very much pleased to see my responsibilities and was eager to retain me for at least three months in Bombay office, since Mr. Rao, Asst Engr of Bombay station was in the notice period and hardly two weeks were left. In this mele, I totally forgot to keep my boss Ex. Engr Shri Bhadury apprised. Actually, all these protocols of office I never took it seriously. Next day as usual I went to Mazagon Dock to meet the MD. Without much pomp and show as usual I went with my blue diary and blue pen. As soon as I entered, I saw a bunch of senior persons with suited booted awaiting their call from the Managing Director of Mazagon Dock. Seeing the crowd, I affirmed myself that I may not get a chance at all to meet him this day. The lady secretary seeing my age and my colour of skin (unlike Marathi's) asked me "Are you from Kerala? I replied, "Madam! if not from Kerala, I am also not far from Kerala." She asked me how? I told her that I have lot of Keralite friends. She enjoyed my conversation and asked me to fill up the slip. The visiting slip had only name, designation and purpose. I filled up and gave her and went to the visitors lounge which was packed. Before I could wipe off my sweat, and settle down a peon came and asked, "Who is Mr. Basu Roy Chowdhury?" All the men started looking at me with raised eyebrows. I went inside and wished the Rear Admiral, who asked me to take my seat. The first thing he noticed was my lengthy name, and then said '" Oh! you are Astt Ex. Engineer from Kandla Port. Now tell me Mr. Basu what is your problem." "I said Sir, I came all the way from Kandla to Bombay to get my ship repaired. I shall feel grateful if you can spare your dry dock". He asked me how many Trawlers I have. I told him '" Sir, only one trawler." He then asked me what is the length of your trawler? I replied, 57 mts. He then picked up the phone and talked to someone and asked me to bring my trawler to drydock no 22, early the next morning. He asked me for how many days and what are the repairs I wanted to do. I said '" Sir, only the hull repair." He further asked if I had fixed a surveyor. I said, "Sir, today itself I shall fix him." He also advised for any other repairs to consult the workshop superintendent Shri Daruwala. I noted down the name and took leave met the Keralan lady secretary, thanked her and left his office. The visitors sitting in the lounge were gazing at me with awe and wonder. The driver asked me," where to sir?" I said MMD office Church gate. Again, I have to meet the Gentleman i.e., Principal Surveyor. Who ragged me the other day nicely. I was a bit nervous. This time I decided, if he starts ragging, I shall fall at his feet and pray for mercy.

Every one of these senior govt officers knew that an Asst Ex. Engineer has to be recruited through UPSC, and without any stuff these candidates are not selected and sent for Central Govt. Assignments, and these junior class I-officers have and enjoy enough administrative and technical powers depending on their postings., so to say there was a great respect for central govt. officers, though they are poorly paid, unlike Pvt sectors. When he heard that I was from Port Blair he took much interest and said, "I am keen to visit Port Blair". He asked me about my educational background, and how I got into this job. I told him, I shall arrange ever thing for him. I remember he also offered me tea and assigned me a surveyor. Getting a surveyor was like getting a lottery ticket as they were in heavy demand. The next day. I thanked him and requested God not to send me again to this place. The next day I took the surveyor to Mazagon Dock no 22, where our trawler M.V. Meena Udyog was docked. The surveyor along with Mazagon dock official was present. He then advised me to get an ultrasonic survey carried out of the Hull plates, the next day, again he visited and marked the plates on the drawing and asked them to remove those plates. There was not much work on the deck side or the engine side / the propulsion side. I dropped the surveyor in his office. He asked me to contact him after the repair was complete, as he has to give a certificate for the sea worthiness of Ship. The propeller of the ship was removed and was taken to the workshop, to see the extent of damage and alignment. In the year 1977, I was amazed to see the huge machine shop of the Mazagon Dock, though I had some idea of a typical marine workshop of Port Blair, where I was a trainee during my college days, but workshop of Mazagon Dock, Mumbai was a superb one and a giant workshop in all sense and a very busy one, and was beyond my imagination. Mazagaon Dock is one of the best dockyards in the country, with huge facilities.

I, came back to Colaba Sassoon harbour relieved my driver Shri Mare and went for lunch. As I returned from lunch the peon of Dr. Radhakrishnan sent a message saying that Ex Engineer Bhadury was in the room of Dr. Radhakrishnan and was waiting to meet me. As I entered his room, Mr. Bhadury asked me as to what was happening, I gave him the total account of my proceedings, but he was bit annoyed as I failed to keep him updated .I told him that ,I kept Dr.Radha Krishnan apprised., but it was my obligation to keep my immediate superior also informed to. Anyway, I apologized and assured him that I would follow the procedure hence forth. Next, Mr. Bhadury advised me to visit the Mazagaon dock daily and ensure that the job is completed as early as possible, because the dock charges in those days were Rs 50.000/- per day. Next, he asked me to give him a written report on the condition of M.V. Kalyani. It was a decommissioning report. He asked me to collect a report of similar vessels from his office and follow the same procedure. Mr. Bhadury then left for his office at Phiroj Shah Mehta Road. The next day I went to Mazagon dock and was there seeing the works of hull repair spent half a day, and then in the afternoon, came to my office and supervised some minor works of Bombay station. While in the office, I started preparing my handwritten report on the decommissioning of trawler M.V. Kalyani. Meanwhile based on my request the Mazgaon officials visited the trawler and inspected the engine and wanted to remove the crank shaft to see the conditions of the main bearing and the connecting rod bearings' Bhadury asked me to get a report and estimate from Mazagaon dock. While the ship was afloat, the crank shaft was removed and taken to workshop to see the condition, and then they put it back for which they charged Rs 10,000.00.

Mr. Bhadury gave the approval and based upon the findings of Mazagaon Dock. I started preparing the report. My daily journey from Andheri Saat (7) Bungalow, to Colaba Sasoon dock, to Mazgaon dock and back to office was moving at a fast pace, when suddenly my boss Mr. Bhadury informed me that our New Director, a marine engineer by profession would visit Bombay station and I should be present. That day I skipped my scheduled visit to M. Dock and remained in the office. The Director visited Bombay office along with Mr. Bhadury had a meeting with Radhakrishnan and while leaving the office Mr. Bhaduri Introduced me, he quickly enquired about my station and the purpose of my visit. Dr Radhakrishnan was kind enough to tell the Director That Mr. Basu has been helping his office, since there was no engineer available for the Bombay station. The Director assured Radhakrishnan to utilize me till such a time an engineer is made available to him. The Director Along with Mr. Bhadury left Bombay office, I went for lunch and as usual left office around 5pm.went back to my guest house and asked the bearer for a cup of coffee, refreshed myself and lied down on by bed fully relaxed. Much to my dismay as the cook checked in with a cup of coffee and two biscuits, he informed me "Aap ka Director Saab aaj guest house may aa gaya. I got a knee jerk and jumped on my bed. Oh! God, what a tragedy?? Why am I required to face this gentle man? It was not palatable news for me. I felt like a fish out of a water. That day I asked the bearer to serve my dinner in my room on the first floor. The next day after returning from office, I asked the guest house attendant, whether the Director checked in and for how many days he would stay here. The attendant informed me that till he gets a house he shall remain in the guest house. I lost all hope and prepared myself mentally to face him. I was locked between the proverbial- **"Devil and the Deep Sea"**. I can't afford to stay outside, nor I would like to face the Director every evening/morning in the dining table, because of the fear of ragging. When I was running between Mazgaon Dock, Sasoon Dock-Colaba, and Andheri –my guest house. After days of hard work and toil, daily I returned to my Andheri guest house like a defeated soldier, getting ready for the next day's battle, not knowing when my journey will end and I shall be able to return back to my base station Kandla. After three weeks of hull repair the trawler M.V. Meena Udyog was taken out of the dry dock, and after certain deck works were completed and released from the Mazgaon dock. The vessel was taken back to Sasoon dock. Now the Insulation work of the fish hold was taken up with the help of local contractors enlisted with Bombay office. The Insulation work took another three weeks and after discussions with my boss I ordered the skipper to set sail for Kandla. The vessel staff was not very keen to return to Kandla, as life in Bombay was too tempting. I stayed back as the de-commissioning report was not ready for submission to the Director. The draft was ready by another two weeks and the handwritten draft was shown to Mr. Bhadury. After getting his clearance I got it typed through one typist of Bombay office. When I look back down the memory lane, I wonder if I missed one golden opportunity in my career. My stay in Bombay office for approximately three months exposed my sincerity, and devotion to all aspects of my dual responsibility as 1) Officer on tour to Bombay for repair of my trawlers and making it seaworthy to sail without knowing anything about the trade. I got firings and was ragged also by my seniors who related to my assignments both directly and indirectly.2) To help Radhakrishnan, Dy. Director of Colaba/Bombay office in handling his day-to-day technical problem, since at this critical juncture, his deputy, i.e., Asst.Engineer(Bombay) had resigned and left. At a very late stage I realized at a dinner with Mr. Bhadury in his residence.as Mr. Bhadury narrated, Dr Radhakrishnan was closely observing my activities in Colaba office and how without any experience and support I neatly winded up my assignments at Bombay and left for Kandla. Seeing my age, enthusiasm and my down to earth approach to all the office staff both technical and administrative Radha Krishnan, pleaded my Boss to talk to Director to retain/transfer me till another Astt Engineer was posted to Bombay office. Radhakrishnan also gave me an option that If I wish I can continue in Bombay Office. But seeing the accommodation crisis and homely food I was enjoying in Kandla, I turned down his request. He also assured me of arranging a two-room quarter generally allotted under Central Gov. pool to the staff of fisheries project staff. For me it was, better an **"egg today than a hen tomorrow"**.

Anyway, at that point of time I was satisfied with my own performance and was elated to know that my position as Asst.Engineer, Junior Class I-Gazette post in the scale was very respectful, and that the experience of three months in Bombay was a god's gift received from the almighty. With All good wishes and blessings, I left Bombay for Kandla, leaving behind the Vessel M.V. Kalyani along with its crew at the Saoon Dock, in Bombay. Clearance was given to the skipper of the repaired vessel M.V. Meena Udyog to set sail for Kandla. On reaching Kandla, Shri Kalachand Chakraborty said my health had deteriorated, and I had fallen sick as I travelled overnight journey after drenching myself in the monsoon rain of Mumbai. After three days of doctors' advice, I recovered from my illness after 7days of rest, I joined my office as usual. From August 1977 the trawler again went out in the Arabian sea for fishing. I became idle again and stared leading a life of "Come day, go day, God send Sunday".

I came to realize that, with this job I shall become a duffer because for the next May 1978, I do not have any work thy name. I started hunting for job through" Employment News "published by Ministry of Labor-the only source in the state govt, central govt and public sector undertaking. Though, I had lot of books in my house, I carried only two volumes of "Mechanical Engineers Hand Book" by KENT a masterpiece reference manual for Mechanical Engineers. I carried these two books and one book which I purchased from the roadside of Bombay's famous Flora Fountain. - "Running and Maintenance of Diesel Engines" one of the best books on diesel engines for a professional engineer, John Lamb, recommended by one ship surveyor of MMD of Bombay during my tour. This book was written by a foreign Marine Engineer, who had spent best part of his life on various ships propelled by diesel engines. This book was a priced possession for me, because I had a terrible interest in Diesel engines, and I considered it as my main forte.

As October approached the Bengalis in Kandla port and Gujaratis of Gandhidham started preparing themselves for Durga Puja and Navratri. I was surprised to see the unique participation of Bengalis and Gujratis in celebrating the festival Durga puja/Navaratri. During the festival, I was feeling very home sick as I was away from my home for the first time during this festival of Bengal, since my childhood. After the festival, I again confined myself to my assignment of Asst Engineer and was thinking how to escape from the current job. As usual winter had set- in at Kandla Port which was close to the Rann of Kachchh and close to Pakistan border on the western front was reeling under chill weather.

During January 1978, I spotted one vacancy in the Employment news for a public sector organization-National Dairy Dev. Board. (NDDB),Anand, an autonomous body under the aegis of Ministry of Agriculture and Irrigation, New-Delhi. I applied for the post of Dy. Engineer, in the same scale of Rs 700-1300/. Within ten days I received a call. Anand was a rail station in Kheda District and was one night journey on Gandhidham Bombay route. I reached Anand the next day and reached the interview venue before time. The interview was taken by the Secretary of NDDB and Director (Purchase). After the interview was over, I was sent to Director (Engineering) a Bengali gentleman, by name Shri Asim Kumar Banerjee. Shri Banerjee also took my interview. The campus of N.D.D.B. was mind blowing, with lush green surroundings, beautiful buildings, everything skip and scan. Really liked the surroundings. The next day morning I reached Gandhidham, without any reservation and obviously, without any sleep. The same day I applied for leave and slept for the whole day. On hearing my story Mr. Chakraborty said "Bose Da –Don't leave this Job, it is a very prestigious post."

Anyway, after taking lunch, I returned back to my room, pondering over my current job. I cannot afford to lose my precious time anymore, how decorated, or prestigious it may be? The appointment letter came within two weeks' time. I was full of joy, as I will be out of my boring life in Kandla. Without waiting for anyone's advice or consent I decided to put in my resignation letter to the Director, Exploratory fisheries Project, Bombay. It took roughly one month for my resignation to be accepted by the Ministry of Agriculture. Once I received the relieving letter, I booked my ticket from Gandhidham to Anand. On 23rdMarch 1978, I Joined NDDB and met Director Engineering Shri Asim Kumar Banerjee. Within a few days, I learnt that during my interview period NDDB recruited about a few hundred engineers from various streams. All fresh engineers were sent for an orientation programme of two weeks. After orientation program, the Director and senior engineers summoned all the fresh engineers-the reason was not known immediately. The Director after initial introduction read out the names of the engineers and their postings in different regional offices and project sites.

Almost ninety percent of the names of fresh engineers were finalized for transfer to the four regions Delhi, Mumbai, Kolkata and Bangalore. My name and other few engineers were left out, I mean they were supposed to work in Head office at Anand. Many of my Bengali engineer friends were happy to get transfer to Eastern Region, Kolkata.

Our Office at NDDB Anand had three important sections viz: a) Engineering Design. b) Dairy Projects (Planning&Execution) and c) Cattle Feed Plant (Planing&Execution). I was asked to sit in the Dairy Plant execution section, which was responsible for execution of all dairy projects under Anand Region. Engineers were busy with all aspects of execution of dairy projects in various parts of Gujarat and Mumbai. I had no idea of a dairy project, so I was sitting idle and passing away my time idly, going to library and occasionally chitchatting with my next table colleagues. After a weeks' time our Director Called me and asked me to join the Tetra Pak Group under a Senior engineer named shri Kulbhushan. I found Shri Kulbhushan a young well-built and a dynamic person, and was incharge of Tetrapak Project, a dream project for NDDB. At the same time The Director called his secretary and asked him to issue an office order posting me permanently in the Tetrapak Project Group.

(Tetrapak is the trade name of a Swedish company, whose tertahedron shaped packet is used for packing aseptic milk, without refrigeration.) In the afternoon as I took my lunch in the canteen and returned to my table, the official order was on my table and within another half an hour, Shri Kulbhushan came and asked me to accompany him, and I became a member of the elite group "TETRA PAK PROJECT."

I found in the group there was another Engineer Shri Chitale. (From Maharashtra). Shri Kulbhushan was from Rajasthan. We were a group of three engineers. Next day I was briefed on the current status of the TETRA PAK PROJECT. It had two important components.

a) Production of Laminated paper.

b) Packing of Ultra High Temperature aseptic milk in Tetrapak containers, which are made of Laminated Paper.

The project feasibility report on Tetra Pack Project was to be submitted to the Ministry of Industry, through our administrative ministry i.e., Agricultural ministry-who would forward the same to the Ministry of Industry, GOI, New Delhi. There was a pressure from the Chairman, NDDB because the Tetrapak project was a dream project of NDDB. In the meantime, the land acquisition was in progress for Installation of the Paper laminating project at Itola, a small station close to Vadodara (Baroda). Simultaneously Delhi's pioneer Architect M/s Kanvinde and Rai were appointed as chief architect responsible for the construction of the Paper Laminating Plant. Meanwhile my boss left for two weeks' visit to Alfa Laval, Lund, Sweden study their Paper Laminating Plant. Shri Kulbhushan, my boss wanted me to learn so many things and asked me to be thorough with each aspect of the project, including civil, electrical and mechanical. Overall, he liked me and took much interest in developing me. The only thing which annoyed him was when I took leave. Within a few months I realized that my boss Shri Kulbhushan was a powerful person and close to the Secretary Shri G.M. Jhala and the chairman Dr. Kurien. Gradually One very senior civil engineer, Mr. Pandya joined our team, because construction work at Itola site was to start soon. Mr. Pandya was to work as site engineer for the project. With in three months' time of my joining, our team was transferred to Baroda. Time kept moving. In the mean while my mother came to Anand along with my room-mate Dr D. K. Roy, who was sharing my room in Anand, and went to Kolkata for some urgent work. While coming back from Kolkata, my mother accompanied her. We all three stayed in Anand for hardly two weeks, when Dr Roy got his transfer order to Himalayan Milk union Darjeeling, West Bengal. I was left alone. Since daily commuting from Anand to Baroda was becoming difficult, my boss insisted that I should shift to Baroda.

Our team moved to Baroda, and after three weeks I managed a house on rent in Baroda.Since April 1977 when I left home for Kandla, I had contact with my parents who were in Barasat, only through letters once a month. But I kept them informed of all important developments taking place till I moved to Baroda with my mother. After a few days the selection committee at Baroda office, selected two electrical engineers and one mechanical engineer for three months of training in Alfa Laval, Sweden. I along with Shri Chitale, P.E. and Shri Shyal Dy.E. from Railways were finally selected, to undergo the training on Tetra Milk packaging plant at Lund ,Sweeden. I had a passport for flying from Port Blair to Calcutta via Rangoon. So, the passport was to be endorsed for visit to Sweden. Other candidates were required to go for Fresh passport. My Boss gave a letter from the M.D. Of Indian dairy Corporation, mentioning my need to visit Sweden, which I produced before the Passport office, Ahmedabad. After Interview. I came back in the evening and within ten days' time, the passport reached the MD's office at Baroda. The year 1978 was coming to an end.

In January 1979, my father wrote to me to come to Kolkata for a week, to select their would-be daughter in law. This time I told my boss that I need to go to Kolkata for a week to settle my marriage. My Boss agreed, I left for Kolkata around 23rd January,1979.

Since my leave was short my father took me to meet the three shortlisted candidates found suitable as my would-be bride.

There was a contrasting difference between my father's and my mother's selection of brides. My father was not very particular about the complexion of the bride, whereas my mother was. My father laid more emphasis on the educational qualification of the bride, whereas my mother's preference was modest education and a fair complexion bride from a good family back ground. My mother's pre-condition of the complexion of the bride prevailed and my father's condition that the bride should possess a master's degree, was also fulfilled. In this case of Mr. Majumdar's daughter. Finally, Mr. Majumdar's daughter, who was an M.A. and was fair complexioned too, was unanimously selected as my final bride.

After a day's rest, as my return journey was fixed, I had to leave Kolkata for Anand. Frankly speaking I had never thought of marrying so soon, because I was dreaming of a good and potential career in NDDB. All my Kolkata friends left one by one. One day casually in an informal get together in 1978, I had asked my Bengali Director Engineering, Shri Asim Kumar Banerjee, as why I was not considered for a transfer to eastern region, when 95% of the engineers got it. My director explained me that, I had performed fairly well in the interview, hence he decided to induct me in a high profile and prestigious project of NDDB i.e.; Tetra Pack Group. While during all my journey time I was dreaming that, since I am not home sick and nor my parents were in favour of calling me to their home town, there was no need to go to Kolkata, sacrificing such lucrative assignment.

In the meantime, my marriage was fixed on 8th May, 1979. Again, I had to take leave and come to Kolkata for my marriage. Frequent leave was not liked by my boss. Since it was marriage, he sanctioned my leave.

My marriage was solemnized on 8th May 1979, at Ballygunge place, in Kolkata. Within a week, I had to leave for Anand as my leave was short. Again, in October after our office shifted to

Baroda and I took a house on rent I had to come to Kolkata to bring my wife who was with her parents in Bhubaneswar.

After a day's rest, it was time to go to Bhubaneswar to my in laws house (for the first time) to bring Lucky (my wife's nick name) to Kharagpur. The only Convenient train then was East Coast Express, which took me to Bhubaneswar around evening. I had the address of my in–laws house at unit- IV, A.G. Colony. On reaching Bhubaneswar I alighted from the train and was looking for a direction to come out of the station. As soon it was known I started walking towards the exit gate when I found that Lucky along with her sister, Saathi and my father-in-law was approaching me, with a peculiar smile on their faces. As a matter of fact, I did not expect such a huge contingent of my in-laws to come to the station for receiving me. I was a bit embarrassed. Any way we came out of the station and took two rickshaws, in which all four of us were accommodated and the rickshaw started moving. For the first time after our marriage, we came physically close to each other and found that my wife and my sister-in-law both were wearing glasses. I was a bit surprised as during my first face to face contact with either of them, there were no sign of spectacles and how come both of them have glasses immediately after the marriage, may be gap of 4-5 months. I asked Maya about this, and she said that she had been using glasses since her college days, and assured me that she would narrate in details after reaching home. After about 15-20 minutes of rickshaw drive we reached Type IV-12, Unit-4, A.G. Colony, Bhubaneswar. Being for the first time in my in Laws company of four members, viz, My wife, Maya, My sister in Law, Saathi and my father in-law and mother in-law I was feeling a bit uncomfortable. Any way my mother-in-law was very happy to receive me and offered tea and snacks and enquired about my programme of stay in Bhubaneswar. I told her that I shall be in Bhubaneswar for two to three days.

During my three days, Lucky was keen to show me all that she could show her husband about Bhubaneswar, the capital town of Bhubaneswar, but during the period she had some M.A. exam papers to be written and was therefore,(despite her eagerness to spend time with me,) she could not do so and therefore I spent the time with Saathi my sister in-law, enquiring about her studies etc. I had casual and relaxed time after couple of months of hectic schedule, after my marriage. Within seven days of our marriage, I had to go back to Anand, my workstation. After three days of stay and visits to Puri, Sun temple, Lingaraj temple, Dhauligiri and Khandagiri, the important tourist spots, we left Bhubaneswar for Kharagpur,where my sister and my brother-in-law, including my nephew Topu were there. The Durga puja in Kharagpur was a dull affair. Immediately after Durga puja festival we left for Baroda. The train was Ahmedabad Express and its arrival time at Kharagpur Railway station was around 11pm. My father, my brother–in-law came to KGP rail station, and we boarded the train and left for Anand. After two nights and one day we reached Baroda, in the evening at around 5p.m. we reached Nagpur Junction.

After reaching Sharad Nagar Society, we went to Chatterjee Babu's house and had dinner. Next Day was Monday, and I was to go to office. Lucky was quick in preparing the meal as well as my tiffin. I was amazed to see how quickly she prepared a square meal for me. My schedule of work resumed, and by 9 am, I used to leave Sharad Nagar and by evening 6 pm returned home. As I returned from office, she used to wait anxiously for me and used to peep through the curtain of the window. In a sense I felt her loneliness.

As days rolled by my father kept pressing me for money, as they were finding it difficult to meet their daily expenditure and house rent with meagre pension of Rs. 250/-, the house rent alone stood at Rs 150/-. With my salary around Rs 900/-, I was too hard pressed to remit every month a considerable amount of Rs 300/-. Ultimately, we decided to seek a transfer to the Kolkata office and accordingly wrote a letter to my engineering Director at Anand, Shri A.K. Banerjee. Shri A.K. Banerjee was initially reluctant as he was the person who probably found in me something positive and put me in the most sought-after engineering project, in NDDB i.e., Tetra Pack. I again wrote back to him requesting him for my transfer. Ultimately my request was conceded, and I was transferred from Baroda, Tetra Pak Project to Eastern Regional Office in Kolkata. Thus, came and end to my long and cherished dream of going abroad. I could have opted for a transfer immediately after joining NDDB, but I did not ask for it. I left it to my Director to decide my future, as I never felt home sick, nor did my parents longed to see their son at home. This was the first time that I relented to her request as I was too soft and did not want to get into any further tussle as partly I and my father were responsible for this financial turmoil. My father arranged my marriage in haste and proved the age old saying **"Marry in haste and repent at Leisure"**.

My parents always wanted to see their son rise in his career, as they found me extremely sincere and duty conscious come what may! After my transfer, Lucky was very happy, but I was not at all as I believed that such a golden opportunity shall not come in my life again. But I strongly believe that I am not going to accept this temporary defeat and that once my responsibility of rehabilitating my parents is over, I shall strike back again. It was a temporary setback and as, I shall have to wait for my next opportunity to strike back again.

I learnt a few hard lessons, which I would like to admit frankly. These are purely my own perceptions and need not be generalized. Barring exceptions, Indian women in general are more concerned about the financial security and are averse to taking risk and not very keen or worried about the career progression of their husband's. Later in this memoir it will be unfolded that my prediction that her family attachment weighed heavily against my rise in my professional career.

Anyway, on the day of my journey from Baroda to Kolkata, my immediate boss shri Kulbhushan Agarwal (who was probably the most disheartened person as my transfer was concerned) and other office colleagues who all bade me **adieu** as my train moved , and rolled on with a jerk , as if reminding me Mr. Basu, this is a lesson for you, for not seeing the future through the eyes of the coin. I could not fathom what was waiting for me in Kolkata and whether I would at all be able to come back to Gujarat to fulfill my lost dream. After 36 hours of journey, we reached Howrah station.

After settling down in NDDB office at Rawdon street, close to Park street, I took charge of the financial portfolio of my family and heard the story from my father and realized that he had made a mess of the whole financial debacle. I concluded the following. My father had no idea or experience of construction of a house in a place like Kolkata and the budgetary needs to complete a house. The plan of the house was too big for a small family like ours and did not suit our pocket. When cement was a controlled item, my father purchased cement at a higher price, thereby wasting a substantial amount of money. The first thing I did was to find out how to get cement from Govt. quota. Second, I sent my father to Andaman to sell our partly finished house and get some cash. I started saving money, each month. Meanwhile Lucky was expecting her first baby. All this along with my tiresome journey of commuting from Barasat(a district head quarters of 24 parganas in West Bengal) to Rawdon Street, office of NDDB daily was a toiling one. With lot of careful planning and extreme control in expenditure, I could help afloat the sinking ship of my father. Virtually I was under a debt trap. But with cautious planning in 1982, I could get cement at a govt. rate, steel rods at a discounted price from rolling mills in Kalyani, stone chips and sand directly from Babu Ghat and finally the roof was casted for our house having a plinth area of approx.1200 sqft. It was a significant achievement and a momentous day for us. Lucky played a key role in foregoing all her personal dreams, in the larger interest of our family, a fact which I admit with all humility.

I shall be failing in my duty if I do not acknowledge her sacrifice at a young age. I could see from a distance that for me, the shore was not far off. Meanwhile the date of delivery for my first child was approaching fast. On November 6th, 1980, Dipa9my first daughter) was born at R.G. Kar Medical College and Hospital, in North Calcutta. Dipa was a beautiful baby, fair complexioned and had a good weight. It was a moment of joy for our family. She was in the hospital for a week and then came back to our rented house in the evening. I was extremely happy and every day after my office hours I used to get impatient as to when I would reach home and see her smiling face. The journey in the evening from Park Street to Barasat(my home town) was a tiring one as in my lifetime I had never undergone such a rigorous commuting. But as proverb goes, I had strong belief that **"God's mill grinds slow**

but sure" I shall overcome this hurdle soon. I saved a fair amount of money, and my father could dispose off our partly built house in Port Blair at a cost of Rs 10,000. There was a big sigh of relief for all of us, as we saved the monthly rent and now that we have a place for our own shelter. We moved into our newly built house, in 1982. As time passed, I was under the physical stress of commuting from Barasat to Park Street as well as the financial burden of complete the balance portion of my house. In between our official residence at Salt Lake was getting ready and in January 1983 we moved to our newly built official residence at Karunamoyee, Salt Lake. Moving from Barasat to Salt Lake was a dream come true as I never expected I would get official accommodation. It was a small but beautiful campus, in Karunamoyee area of Salt Lake. In January 1983, I packed all our belongings and hired a truck and came to Salt Lake to take possession of our Flat no D7 which was on the fourth floor. Salt Lake then (in 1983) was thinly populated. After unloading all our furniture, we returned back to Barasat. Since Lucky and Dipa were in Bhubaneswar, I had to travel up to Bhubaneswar to bring them back. On reaching Salt Lake Lucky, was terribly excited to see her new accommodation at Salt Lake.

. All our family members including my in laws were very happy to see us settled in Kolkata. In January 1983 we moved to Salt Lake, then came Durga Puja in October 1983. Many of our relatives also came to see our campus including my sister and brother-in-law. There was a Jheel Meel park with a toy train, now it is renamed Nicco Park. It was a cock-a-hoop, but who knew that dark clouds were hovering over my head. As we were enjoying the winter of 1983, Dipa's birthday approached on 6th of November, and we invited almost all the children of NDDB campus. My parents also came and took part in the celebration. As we moved into the new year of 1984, it was celebrated along wth our new Director,Shri A. K. Banerjee ,who was Director in NDDB ,Bangalore. Our Park Street office moved to Karunamoyee Salt Lake and we finally settled in salt lake with our residential complex being about 200m away from our residence. After a long battle of commuting from Barasat for almost 3years, I heaved a sigh of relief. Suddenly, as it is proverbial, there is always a calm before a storm, in a like way there was a big blow to engineers of NDDB Salt Lake office, when in May 1984, there was a mass transfer from NDDB Kolkata, to different office in NDDB spread all over the country. The axe also fell on me, and I was transferred to NDDB, H.O.at Anand, Gujarat. The transfer order came to us on our anniversary day i.e., 8th May. Excepting me, everyone was upset about my transfer. Gradually, we started packing our furniture, arranging for transport, insurance etc. Finally, and we boarded our train Ahmedabad Express for our journey to Anand. At station came our Senior friend cum office colleague, Shri Asim Kumar Datta. After almost 36hours of Journey, we reached Anand around evening. Shri H.C. Sikdar, who was then with NDDB, Anand, booked guest house for us at Anand. We moved to guest house, and in the same day evening, we had our dinner at Sikdar Da's house at Ankur Society, behind NDDB campus. Lucky had slight temperature, because of the tiring journey from Kolkata to Anand.

Next day evening, I was glancing at the notice board of NDDB, when our Director (Engg) shri D.K. Sen came down from the lift. I wished him and informed him about my arrival. He advised me to meet him the next day in his office. Next day as I met him, I came to know that I have been transferred to Bharuch Dairy Project, a project site in a small district, between Surat and Baroda. Though I was not happy with this transfer but at the same time, I could not protest before the Director, as I was meeting him for the first time. Mr. Sen asked me as to how soon I can move to the project site? I told him that my luggage was on the way and unless the truck reaches Anand I shall not be able to move out of Anand. Shri Sen handed over the transfer order and asked me to go through the Drawings of the Project, as the Mechanical & Electrical installations have already started. Within a few days the truck reached Anand and I arranged for its redirection from Anand to Bharuch. We on our part took a small matador. Lucky, Dipa and me boarded the matador, with our small baggage and left for Bharuch. At Bharuch dairy site there was a civil site engineer, who received us and we moved into a quarter which was almost ready, excepting interiors. Next Day, our redirected truck reached Bharuch site and all the goods were unloaded and moved into our residence. From May 1984 to December 1985, we remained at Bharuch Dairy site and Dipa got admitted in Gujrat Narmada Fertilizers Company (GNFC) English medium school, which was a missionary, Kinder garden school within the campus of GNFC. GNFC was a huge fertilizer complex and was probably the only fertilizer company at Bharuch District, Gujarat.

At site, while the erection of plant and machinery was in progress, I learnt lot of lessons on Dairy plant Execution and management. My senior engineers were also happy with my hard work and dedication. There was lot of freedom at site and there was a provision of site allowance, and lot of financial and administrative powers were delegated to the site engineer. While the work was on the verge of completion my senior project engineer shri S. K. Garg once casually asked me if I was interested in doing a project work (as site engineer) on powder plant, which was coming up at Godhra a small town about 50 kms towards Anand on the national highway. He also told me that my Director, Mr.

Sen particularly wanted me to handle this project, under the overall supervision of a foreign consultant, [FAO(Rome)]. I told Mr. Garg that I need some time to decide on this. There was also an expansion of dairy capacity at Godhra dairy project. The work of installation of a spray drying plant was in fact a supplement to the expansion plan, which was being executed by H.O. at Anand. I came home and told Lucky about the proposal and my keen desire to do the project so that I can make up the loss (of seniority) of almost 5years in N.D.D.B. The only problem at that time was Dipa's education as she had attained the age of four and was ready for admission to class I, in any school. At Anand there were two schools, an English medium school and the other was a Central school. Our choice was Central School as our service was transferrable. The English medium School used to accommodate students round the year, whereas it was difficult though not impossible to take admission in central school in the mid of session.

For the intervening period she can go to 'Boho Sishu Vihar' a Nursey school run by the ladies of NDDB inside Anand Campus. After lot of arguments and counter arguments, I had to surrender before Lucky and decided that I shall turn down the request, when Mr. Garg, visits next time to Bharuch. As usual before winding up the Bharuch dairy project Mr. Garg came to see, whether I could be transferred back to Anand and was but naturally keen to know my reaction. When Mr. Garg asked me about my decision, I told him that since my daughter was to be admitted in Central school, I may be exempted from a second transfer to Godhra Dairy Project. Mr. Garg in front of another Sr.Engineer told me that Mr. Sen would be disappointed to hear this ,as he was hopeful about my decision. With folded hands I requested Mr. Garg to kindly consider my request, as I was contemplating that if an order is issued against my wish, I shall have no option left, but to join

Godhra Dairy Project. In the evening Shri Garg left for Surat, to attend another site meeting.

Evening, I came back to my residence, with a heavy heart, recalling the day when in 1980 I had to quit the Tetrapak Project and had to move to Kolkata, against the wish of the then Director (Engg) Shri A.K.Banerjee. Now I realize that if a person has to climb up the ladder in his professional career, cooperation and sacrifice of his family is a must. The same evening, I tried to push in my justification before Lucky, that I missed another golden chance of a lift in my career. Somehow, I failed to convince Lucky that bosses are instrumental in making or damaging your career. From that day I concluded that I lost my professional battle in NDDB and that I should look for other avenues. Even today while writing this memoir, I recall that for professional men serving in any position like me, golden opportunity comes only once in a lifetime, but for me God gave me two chances, but sadly I could not avail both the chances. For the first one, I blame myself and my father, as both of us never thought of financial planning, in the early years of my career, otherwise there was no reason as to why I should quit the opportunity and opt for a transfer just to save me and my family from a financial catastrophe. For the second one, when Director Shri Sen picked me as his favorite candidate for installation of powder plant in NDDB, I failed to convince Lucky that for achieving big things in life you need to sacrifice small things. Just let us take a calculated risk. Dipa's admission was possible in any school in Godhra (Godhra, I was told by shri Garg that Godhra had a Central school) or in Anand as Godhra was close to Anand, but regrettably she did not give me any chance to negotiate the deal with NDDB. She could have stayed in Anand while on weekends I could have visited Anand from Godhra. After the Bharuch Dairy project was completed, I was called back to

Anand and was posted in Engineering Division. Again, after my posting at Anand Engineering Division I was sent for a one month's training at Sabar Dairy, which was a 4 lakh litres/ day Dairy, and situated in Sabarkantha district of Gujarat. I was under the impression that probably Director Shri Sen was happy with my work at Bharuch Dairy and was grooming me for some big dairy project. For about three weeks, I stayed in a hotel and after whole days of work, I used to prepare hand sketches and notes for each section of this large dairy plant. After the training I brought the Double Foolscap notebook with every detailing/drawing from civil, electrical and mechanical angle, as well as dairy technology what an engineer ought to know about a dairy project specially, about the planning and execution part, and to be more specific, what a consultant engineer should know know. After coming back to Anand, I met Shri Sen and showed him my assignments and drawings I learnt from Sabar dairy. At that point of time there was a rumor that NDDB was planning a modern dairy at Gandhinagar, the Secretariat or administrative capital of Gujarat. Since I was without any portfolio, I used to spend much of my time in the library collecting notes from foreign journals associated with Dairy and books pertaining to dairy. My only aim was to master the dairy field and to cover up my(lost) golden years in NDDB Kolkata.

Here, one thing I should admit that, while I was a Junior Engineer in Port Blair or Asst. Engineer at Kandla port my domain of Technical knowledge was restricted to Diesel engines or Diesel Power plants only, but in NDDB, I was exposed to many areas of engineering viz;Substations, Refrigeration plants, Effluent treatment plants, milk processing plants etc. The milk processing plant in itself was a very vast subject, especially powder plants. From January 1986 till May 1986, generally I remained without any portfolio. There after summer had set in and we planned to go to Kolkata for a month's leave. After returning from Kolkata, I was told by my next table colleague in the Engineering Division that, I had been transferred to Purchase Division . The next day I received my Official order, which was **a bolt from the blue**, because I had the passion to work in the Engineering Division and never expected to work in purchase division as , I considered it as more of a clerical job, which does not require much technical knowledge. I had no choice and with my transfer order, in hand I went to meet the Director, Purchase Division, who was in a departmental meeting, with his officers. The day I refused Mr. Sen's request to take up the Godhra project, I knew I had not been in his good books. Shri Gore welcomed me and offered me a seat in the purchase office. I continued working in the purchase division from 1985 to 1990. In the year 1989, I had repeated attacks of Malaria, when I met the M.D. of NDDB and requested for a transfer to eastern region on medical grounds. My request was considered, and I was transferred to Kolkata office. On 7th May,1990 my second daughter Rupa was born. This was a turning point in my life. My life both in the office and domestic front changed dramatically.

Unlike purchase division in Anand life was tough and hectic in Eastern Region, besides there were lot of project sites under my control, where frequent visits were to be made for supervising the progress and to deal with technical problems. Since I had completed one dairy project in Bharuch, I had technically no difficulty in managing the projects. During the period from May 1990 to 1995, when we moved from Salt Lake to IIT-Kharagpur, many memorable incidents took place in my /our life. some of them are appended below.

On 11th March 1993, my father in- law late Anil Kumar Majumdar, suddenly breathed his last. This was a terrible shock to Lucky, my wife being the elder daughter and being very affectionate to her father. Saathi (Banani) the younger daughter, who is a Doctor, and my brother-in-law Dr Goutam Bose were in Agartala, the capital town of Tripura. Both were informed but could arrive only in the evening. Consequently, I had to perform the last rites. Subsequently the responsibility of taking care of my mother in-law came on Lucky's shoulder. Her family pension, arrangement of a tenant for the stand-alone house also was arranged inter-alia other domestic responsibilities. I took LTC (Leave Travel Concession) and took my mother-in-Law to Port Blair in October 1993 during Durga puja Break, for a change. I left Port Blair (my birth place) in 1977 and after almost 16 years again visited the islands, with old and beautiful memories. My Uncle (Choto Mama) Shri Dilip Kumar Ghosh was then Superintendent, in the same Electricity Board from where I Left Port Blair. My uncle came to harbour to receive us, and we drove straight to his residence. No sooner had we reached there, than the news of our arrival spread like a wildfire. I took Lucky and my mother-in-law to all the important places including Corbyn's Cove a tourist and a swimming beach site in open sea, as also Jolly Bouy, where you can see the corals in the sea through a glass boat. The journey from Port Blair to Jolly Bouy was just like Ritwik Roshan film and song **"Kaho Na Pyaar Hai"**. In midst of all these events, Rupa fell sick and had stomach infection and we had to cut short our tour and return to Kolkata by the next available ship. All my friends and acquaintances and college friends were very much delighted to see me and invited us for Lunch / Dinner. It was a very pleasant and refreshing memory. We returned to Kolkata, by ship M.V. Nicobar, a luxury passenger liner. In midst of busy schedule, time was running like a speeding boat rolling and tossing and cutting across all waves of a middle-class orthodox family. Suddenly in the month of the same year ie; 1993 my father, who had maintained excellent health throughout his life suddenly became serious and one day he started vomiting blood. Our tenant who was staying with my parents informed me over the phone and I rushed to see him in Barasat, Dist. hospital. The case was referred to Calcutta Medical College and he was admitted there. At this juncture, I saw how my father was neglected and almost forced to die after the third day of admission. Since I did not have enough money, I had to watch silently and helplessly my father succumb to his illness. It was 14th December 1993, that my father breathed his last. After completing all rituals, I joined my office after almost two weeks of break. My sister & brother-in-law, who were in Kharagpur were also present during the mourning period as per tradition. We returned to Salt-Lake leaving my mother in the care of our tenant. Barasat was only 20 kms from Salt Lake, and I used to visit frequently. At the office front, all the projects under my control in Bihar were gradually coming to an end. In the office front my immediate boss, Shri Subhas Chander was a Haryana man, and did not like my sitting in office. **I decided mentally that I have two options before me: -**

- If I am to continue in NDDB, I must upgrade my technical knowledge. which was crucial for my next promotion.

- Alternately, I must change my role from technical to managerial, because as my own perception, I was professionally more competent as a manager than as an engineer.

Meanwhile a new development was taking shape. A new Metro dairy project of 4LLPD (lakh litre per day) was coming up at Barasat, Subhas Nagar not very far from my house, Barasat and I decided that I should get a berth in this project as a manager or as an engineer.

One thing I strongly believed in my life, that if I work sincerely, I should be rewarded. ***God helps those who help themselves.*** In 1994, I moved out of my comfortable office life at Salt Lake and started camping in my house in Barasat along with my mother and started going to the project site and used to go back to Salt Lake after every three days. This continued for one and half years and I learnt a lot of technical things, which were not there in my basket. At times I used to question myself, as to why I am taking all these troubles? The answer I got was, at this age of 43 years it was hard if not impossible to get a new job and that if my destiny was to continue with NDDB, I should continue living with dignity. I wanted to master both theorical and practical aspects of all the technical issues that cropped up. Another development which further reinforced my desire to quit NDDB was that, as time passed on, I continued struggling my daily battle of commuting from Salt Lake to Metro dairy to my house at Barasat and then back to Salt Lake. Gradually I was honing my technical knowledge. The year 1995 approached with some good news. My elder daughter stood first in Salt Lake Central school combining all the three sections. This was great news for us. Now she moved from class IX to class X. The Barasat Dairy was nearing completion, and the work was in full swing. The problem of induction of my younger daughter Rupa into Central school became important, and Lucky was a bit concerned. We tried other private schools in and around Salt Lake area but somehow, she could not compete and therefore we were left with no other choice, but to go for class I in Central school. Getting admitted in Central school proved tough. The day the final list appeared, I came running from Barasat Metro dairy, straight to the school to find that she was kept in waiting list number 1. Ultimately, she got the seat and was admitted in KV-1, Central school at Karunamoyee, Salt Lake. Except Barasat Metro Dairy and Expansion of Existing Mother Dairy at Dankuni, there were no other projects, in Eastern Region. Engineers from our office were being gradually transferred from NDDB Eastern Region to other regional offices. I was a bit relaxed as, both my daughters were in Kendriya Vidyalaya. In the month of June 1995, after the results were declared, Dipa, my elder daughter moved to class X and Rupa also got admission in Class I. Both started attending central school in Salt Lake. During August 1995, there appeared an advertisement for Dy. Registrar (purchase) in IIT –Kharagpur. IIT-Kharagpur, being an Institute of National Importance and was directly under the Ministry of HRD, I felt that it was the most appropriate organization and time for me to join, provided I am selected. Since I had good knowledge about indigenous and foreign purchase and I wanted a permanent job in West Bengal, I thought of applying. By the grace of God, I was selected. The scale of Deputy registrar (in IIT-KGP) at that point of time was equivalent to that of Dy Manager in NDDB. In NDDB I was Project Engineer, the next was Sr. Project Engineer and then Dy. Manager. So, the post of Dy Manager (scale was equivalent to that of Dy. Registrar in IIT-KGP. The day I got my appointment letter, I met my Regional Director and told him that I am now out of Bond of Serving NDDB. He shook hands and congratulated me saying that *"Basu, Tumne Kar Dikhaya"* meaning that you have done it. In the farewell address he also mentioned my grit and determination to quit NDDB. The final offer letter came in August, and I joined IIT–KGP on 9th October1995, after completing all formalities in NDDB. My only worry was whether

Dipa will be allowed to appear for her class X Board Exam from IIT-KGP as the forms for admit cards were being filled in. I immediately rushed to Kharagpur, Central school and met the Principal and came to know that the process of filling out forms for Class X Board exam 1996 was in progress. The teacher-in-charge (EXAMS) and the principal assured me that there will be no problem. The last date was around 20th October 1995. This was a great relief for me.

PART THREE

From 9th October to 31st May 2011

...

Leaving a long journey of seventeen years of career in NDDB and joining IIT-Kharagpur an institution created by late Dr. Bidhan Chandra Roy a visionary leader, a statesman, and an Architect of modern Bengal.I joined IIT-KGP on 9th Oct,1995. Thus, I began a new journey in my life. I thanked God for saving me from professional humiliation and the tension and hassle of transfers and getting my both kids admitted in Central schools. A new phase of my life began, and I decided to concentrate on my job and gradually earn the respect and confidence of the Director, Dy. Director (my immediate boss) and the Registrar.It is important for me as well as the readers to know about what IIT-Kharagpur is, besides an institution of higher learning. We are all aware that IIT's are pool of our country's best technical brain, and IIT-Kharagpur is the mother of all IIT's.

When Late Pandit Jawaharlal Nehru wanted to build an institute, which would nurture the best brains and train them to be of service to the nation, he consulted Late B.C. Roy the then Chief minister of West Bengal.At the advice Of Late B.C. Roy, Pandit Ji agreed to establish the Institute in Kharagpur.

My wife Lucky was not very happy to leave a place like Salt Lake and move to a place which was calm and quiet and relatively out of din and bustle of a metro city. Dipa got her admission in IIT-KGP Central school and filled her form for 1996 Board Exam of CBSE, and Rupa got admission in St. Agnes, convent school. Both the schools were located inside the campus, so there was no tension as far as the education of my daughters were concerned. After joining IIT-KGP I had a relatively quiet life in the office, no tours, travels, humiliation by immediate boss. There was a heap of responsibility, but my bosses were extremely polite and helpful and guided me properly in discharging my responsibilities effectively. They were all senior professors and loved me because they came to know that I was a graduate Mech. Engineer.

After joining IIT-KGP, my mission now was to concentrate my focus on Dipa's academic career. No sooner had she joined Kendriya Vidyalaya, the very next day her flock of friends barged into our house, I was shocked to see them and was wondering, as to how, so soon she could have such large number of friends. Dipa's nature was such that everybody loved her, teachers, friends, neighbors, everyone. She was smart, helpful, and talkative, but very childish too, and was frank in her dealings.

One incident which I can't forget, was her first parent teachers meet (PTM) immediately after her pre-board examination, in IIT-KGP around December 1995. I went to the school and occupied the last bench, as all the faces were new to me, both students and parents. When all the parents had finished seeing their answer scripts, one parent asked the English teacher as to who did score the highest mark in English, the teacher pointed his finger to wards Dipa. The teacher then told the gathering that she

(Dipa) had recently joined on transfer from K.V. Salt lake-I. I remember one or two parents wanted to see the answer script of Dipa, which was allowed by the teacher, and after seeing the answer script, they were spell bound. We came to IIT-KGP in October1995, and by December 1995 she had established her base (as a good student) in K.V. It was a great moment for me. Then came the final class X Exam in March 1996.The exam went off smoothly and the results were declared in June 1996. She scored 82% marks in aggregate and in math her score was 95/100. There was a problem in math on Trigonometry, (Heights and Distances chapter) and the problem was related to calculate the height of a balloon, which she could not attend correctly, as a result five marks assigned to the problem was missed by her. Otherwise, she did all other problems correctly. I personally knew that Dipa had prepared so well in mathematics that there was no reason as to why she should not have scored 100/100.

This incident was so memorable that even today after almost after 25 years, I share with family members about the ***famous Balloon problem*** of class 10 Board exam. Immediately after the exam the students of her class decided to go for JEE coaching, with the resources available within the campus. For Physics coaching, all the girls assembled in our house and our house was selected by the Physics teacher for coaching every Sunday. Likewise, another student's residence was selected for Chemistry and Math was held in the house of Math teacher itself. Dipa was continuing with her coaching while Rupa was gradually progressing in St. Agnes School within the campus. Ultimately, the day came when Dipa was ready for her final class 12 exam. We were very tense, but the exam went off smoothly. As far as Coaching is concerned, IIT KGP did not have any professional coaching Centre. At any rate I was not very keen about Dipa's getting into IIT, as I never wanted her to stress beyond a certain point as she was not keeping very good health, as demanded from a student preparing for IIT JEE. She appeared in it as well for JEE (West Bengal). IIT-KGP results were out and she could not clear it, I was not at all upset. In the meantime, I had to look for admission to normal colleges, in West Bengal. To the best of my memory I had searched every nook and corner of the city of Calcutta for her admission to a normal college in Calcutta for a major course in mathematics, but I failed .One prime reason was the colleges in West Bengal treated other board(CBSE) candidates as academically inferior to candidates from other Boards and used to rate them with a deduction of 10% of their total marks obtained. Besides Dipa Scored on an average 75% marks, which was not up to our expectation. Since all academic doors in Calcutta were virtually closed for Dipa, I had to take her to Kalyani University, for admission to BCA course, by filling the form and completing all formalities. We left Kharagpur early in the morning and returned from Kalyani around 4pm in the evening, by train. Dipa was limping with a corn in her leg. After reaching Sealdah station, we walked down and reached NRS medical college to see the results of WBJEE. The list of successful candidates was displayed on the notice board, the visibility of which was so poor that I could not read properly and left it to Dipa. After thoroughly checking the long list Dipa told me with a blank face that she was not there. I was also shocked and asked her to look at the list once again carefully, but Dipa confirmed that it was not there. Any way I was also mentally disturbed and could not utter anything. From NRS Medical college we boarded a bus for Garia heading towards my in-law's house, for a day's stay. After reaching Garia we narrated the whole episode to my mother-in-law. Next day morning, we left for Kharagpur, we reached home and told the story to Lucky. Meanwhile lucky was keeping a close eye on Newspaper about academic announcements and told us about the BSc, B.Ed programe under Utkal University. Immediately we got Dipa's biodata typed and sent it to the Principal of the College. My office colleague, in accounts whose son was classmate of Dipa informed about the form submission in Midnapore College, which was a very old college for science stream. The next day we went to Midnapore college, filled in the form, submitted, and returned. My Professor friend Prof. S. K. Basu informed me about the Gope College (women college)in Midnapore, where they are seeking admission for science stream. Immediately next morning, we went to Midnapore women's college popularly known as Gope college.

Within a week's time someone from my office informed that the admission to first year science stream was going on and Dipa's name was on the college notice Board. Since I had an urgent meeting, I requested my superintendent Ray Babu to organize the trip to Midnapore. Ray Babu immediately summoned a vehicle from our automobiles section and asked one staff from our office and sent to my residence to pick up Dipa and Lucky and the vehicle straight away drove to Gope College Midnapore. Dipa got her admission for BSc (Maths Hons) in the college as well as hostel, completed all formalities and by evening 6p.m., they returned. Dipa and her mom were looking very happy and I, on my part, heaved a sigh of relief. Next day I went to the office and told my friends and colleagues that Dipa got admission in Gope college in BSc (Math Hons). I was told that Gope Women's College was under Midnapore University and had a good reputation as a girl's college.

Since Dipa was extremely good in math, I wanted her to pursue a career in math. I also planned in my own way once that after her graduation in Math (Hons), she will appear for MSc (Math) lateral entry exam of IIT Kharagpur and then after completing her MSc, she would do her PhD in math. This was my plan. I was confident that with her mathematical brain and my extremely good relations across IIT KGP, I shall be able to find a berth for her to pursue studies in IITKGP and ultimately see her receiving a degree from this famous Institute, on a convocation day wearing her convocation attire in front of the famous statue of late Dr. B. C. Roy the founder father of IIT-KGP.

After watching so many convocations at IIT-KGP, I always felt that if so many students can get their degree from IIT-KGP, why not Dipa?? Thus, I did not know that I was daydreaming, which later fell flat. There is a word called destiny, which was not in my hands. Here I would like to say a few words. Every parent (generally) aspires to fulfill their unfinished dream, through their children. In my case my dream was to study in IIT-Kharagpur, but I could not make it. But having seen the meteoric rise in her academic achievements, I decided to take a chance and I was more than confident that Dipa would make it. Next was our trip to Gope college hostel because the following week her classes would start. We all went to the hostel with Dipa's bedding and other sundry items, and Lucky saw her hostel, met the lady Warden and we returned. Dipa was in tears and so was her mom, I too felt emotional as she was out of house for the first time. After spending two weeks Dipa said she cannot stay in that hostel on two counts, standard of food and unhygienic conditions of hostel washrooms. We decided to withdraw her and put her in a private women hostel in and around Midnapore, after Puja. Meanwhile she, along with my friend Prof. B.B. Ghosh's (Professor in Mech Engg Dept) daughter decided to commute from IIT-KGP to Gope college on daily basis, along with Prof S. K. Basu's daughter. All the three students were studying with math as their major subject. This continued and Dipa was happy with the teaching faculty of Mathematics Department, and she got fully absorbed in her studies. After a month's class, puja vacation started and we decided to go to Puri for a break Mean while before Dipa appeared for her board exam I got a book on Private Engineering college from IIT-KGP and went through it thoroughly. Since, those days Pvt Engineering colleges were not many in West Bengal students started migrating to Bangalore and Nagpur, where there was large no of Pvt. Engg colleges. Many of my friends in IIT-KGP, suggested to take Dipa to Bangalore but I did not venture as I was not very conversant with the state and the state was too far from Bengal. But then after reading the handbook, I found the Rating of Vellore Engineering College (VEC) was very good, but the college was away from Madras on way to Bangalore. Casually, I sent a Registered Letter to the Registrar for a copy of the Prospectus. No sooner we returned from Puri, I found the prospectus of VEC lying in our house. I went through the prospectus and appreciated the style in which the details of the college were presented. After some discussion I decided to call the Registrar and find out if there were some seats vacant as the admission session was already over by then. The Registrar told me that there were some seats left in Civil, Chemical and other branches and advised me to come to Vellore quickly in case I was interested. Since I studied in Annamalai university for five years, I knew Tamil Nadu very well and had no hesitation in taking Dipa to a state, with which I was familiar. After getting confirmation from the Registrar VEC, we started our maiden journey to Vellore, through a puja special train with the name of

God. We reached Madras Central the next day evening. The train for Vellore (Brindavan Express) was the next morning. We spent our night at Madras Central, the next day got tickets and boarded Kovai express. The train was packed and we had to stand for virtually three hours. We got off at Katpadi station, took an auto and left for a city hotel in Vellore. After boarding a hotel, we took masala dosa and took tea and went for a nap. We were tired because the whole night we could not sleep and in Brindavan expressed for three hours we kept standing.

The next day we took an auto and with bedding, suitcase, bucket etc., we went straight to the college and met the Registrar. The Registrar was a nice person and within a few hours all formalities, including hostel accommodation, was provided. Her admission was confirmed in the Chemical Engineering Department. Over the telephone the Registrar requested the Lady warden to provide accommodation to Dipa. We had lunch in the staff canteen and moved to the hostel. Dipa checked in and returned after some time and confirmed that the rooms, washrooms were pretty good, and she was very happy and was full of excitement. At around 3pm I left the college after visiting the library. Next day After taking lunch in the afternoon, I went to the college and met all the first-year teachers and requested them to look after Dipa as she joined a bit late in the college. I also visited the workshop, met the Foreman, and requested him to take care of her, as the mechanical workshops are a bit difficult for girl students, Dipa being physically a bit weak. All the teachers and technical staff were very happy, knowing that we came from Kolkata, and assured me that they would take care of her. No sooner, she joined her college, friends started encircling her like a honeybee. I went to the hostel to see her off, as I had to leave for Chennai. I saw her going to her workshop practical with green workshop gown. I asked her from where she got it. She replied her roommate gave her as it was mandatory to wear workshop gown for workshop practical. After talking for a minute or two, I bade goodbye to Dipa and moved towards the canteen, took lunch and boarded a bus for Chennai. By road it was four hours run from Vellore to Chennai. I got down at Mount Road and took an auto and went straight to Madras Central station. My train Madras Howrah mail was scheduled to leave at 10pm. I took Dinner at Railway catering and boarded the train. I had a reserved ticket from Vellore through a travel agent. As the train gushed and roared, I heaved a sigh of relief, alas! I could get her admitted in a good engineering college. She got chemical engineering branch. I was sure that, I need not look back, as far as academic progress was concerned. My only responsibility is that I have to pay the fees (which were high) regularly at the beginning of each semester. After reaching IIT-KGP, I narrated the whole story to Lucky and she was very happy about her college. Time rolled by and we all (including Rupa) visited Vellore in the Year 2000,when she was in second year. By then it was academically known to all that she had excelled in her department. I met all the Professors and all of them were happy with her performance. I even heard one of her Professors, once commented in his class, that if any student deserves admission in MIT, USA, it was only Jayita Basu. Her academic grade card also reflected her performance. In her final year of study her project guide was an Associate professor, and was working on a consultancy project from Ministry of Science and technology .The Professor got all the spade work done through Dipa for his project. While she worked very hard she got infected with Jaundice and her health was going down, when her mother was in mood to go to Vellore and stay there ,so that she could cook for her homely dishes. The idea was dropped as Dipa gradually recovered. During her final exam (last phase) Lucky went to Vellore to help Dipa wind up her stay in Vellore and said goodbye to Vellore and returned to IIT-KGP, by Coromandel Express in the scorching heat of summer 2002.During her third-year exam she was interviewed by Cognizant Technologies and was selected, but appointment letter was not forthcoming. After Reaching Kharagpur I had a doubt whether ultimately, she would receive it or not? After joining IIT-KGP, I had always cherished that Dipa should get a degree from IIT-KGP, because I saw so many students of IIT, I wondered why Dipa, can't get a degree from IIT. I used all the resources I had at my disposal as a senior officer of IIT administration, I tried to see if Dipa could get a birth in M. Tech, through project mode. Since she was a chemical engineer and had Industrial training in Dairy Industry (Barauni Dairy), I thought Food and Dairy engineering (Under the Department of Food and Dairy Engineering) would be ideal for her. At the same time I started meeting Professors for direct entry to PhD, as there was a provision that if a student gets 60% marks in B.Tech he/she can directly register for PhD, subject to interview clearance by the DSC (Doctoral Scrutiny Committee). At the same time, I also got a professor friend in chemical engineering who agreed to coach her for GATE exam. I also took Dipa to Jadavpur University for direct admission to M.E. in Chemical engineering, through project mode. Accordingly, she also appeared for an interview for research Assistant in a project under IIT Rural Development Centre. At any rate I wanted her to get engaged either in job/studies. After the interview in IIT-KGP was over, I asked the Chairman of the Committee Prof. S. K. Lahiri (who was also my boss) about her performance. Prof. Lahiri commented, "I did not know that she was your daughter, but she is very intelligent and has performed extremely well".

Please don't ask me whether she will be selected or not, that I can't say". Ultimately, she was selected. and got an offer for Rs 5000 per month, sitting at home. Not a bad deal! Through this project mode you can learn and earn an M.S. degree. You can earn an M.S. as well as PhD also. From Jadavpur University also she got a call (after applying for it against newspaper advertisement) to appear for an interview for selection to the M.E degree. There was only one seat, for which there were around sixty to seventy candidates from different colleges. The Chemical Engineering Department of J.U. is very famous and is well known to the academic world. I concluded; it is not possible for her to fight against a lone seat. Any way we Left KGP early in the Morning and reached J.U. by 10 am. The interview room was full of candidates. The interview started at 11am.When her turn came, I started walking along the corridor, and watched her replying to all questions, that were barged at her by the panel of professors. After the interview we left the campus and took it for granted that unless something miracle happens, my dream of admitting her on an M.E. course will remain as a dream only. After a few days my staff had gone to Kolkata for some work, visited J.U .Chemical engineering Dept, and found that her name was second in the merit list .The first was also a lady candidate of J.U. who had some industrial experience got some weightage, and got to the top position in the merit list .Immediately, I ran to J.U. and met the HOD of Chem Engg. and discussed the issue. The HOD told me that if the first candidate does not turn up then only, she has a chance. He asked me to wait for another one week, by when the situation will be clear. Next week I met the HOD again when he confirmed that the first candidate did not turn up ,so Dipa was selected and asked me to meet the Superintendent. Of P.G. for admission formalities. **That day was the happiest moment**

in my life. I immediately informed Dipa by calling up her over the phone. In the evening I returned home, and we shared that joyous moment with my family members. I thanked God for showering her blessings on Dipa. Next day we went to J.U. for formal admission, though the admission formalities were completed but, she could not get accommodation in the hostel, as hostel facilities were extended only for students outside the city of Kolkata. Any way we decided to put her in a PG accommodation immediately after Durga puja which was a matter of one month. The classes were to start in another weeks' time. She decided to commute from Barasat, where my mother was staying alone. In the meantime almost daily, I used to contact the HRD manager of Cognizant Technologies in Chennai for her appointment letter, but unfortunately there was no positive response from their end. As a matter of fact I was not very worried about her job prospects, as I believed she had a lot of potential and that she can herself fetch a job, and does not require anybody's help. Let her complete her master's degree and once she obtains a master's degree she will have three options before her :

- Go for higher studies in any foreign country.
- Go for a teaching assignment.
- Go for a job other than teaching.

She started attending her M.E. classes and was full of praise of the teaching faculty of J.U. After attending three weeks of classes at J.U. one fine morning I got a call from Cognizant Technology, asking us to come to Chennai to complete her appointment formalities. Lucky was very happy, but I was not. We boarded Madras bound special train and checked into a hotel on Waltex road, by the side of Madras Central station. The medical examination went off and within another two days the appointment letter was issued with a group lunch for the new appointees. The moment we landed in Madras, I was running high and dry as to where to keep Dipa, because I was sure she would get a berth in CTS (Cognizant Technology Solutions). There were other girls from Kerala, but they formed a group among themselves, and arranged some accommodations, leaving Dipa alone. I tapped all my resources (when I was a student way back in 1970) but now Chennai has changed a lot. Anyway, everyday morning after having breakfast we started roaming in Chennai city for suitable accommodation but could not find any proper accommodation. I was a bit disappointed. One brilliant idea stuck me: -

1) First locate the Bengali Association, meet the Secretary, and seek help.2) Locate Ramakrishna Centre and find where the ladies' hostel is located in the city and meet the warden and seek her help. Because in Kolkata there is a ladies hostel in Entally, where my sister,Rekha stayed and completed her B.Sc programme. Both the ideas worked out. The Madras Bengali Association which is located in T.Nagar was known to me when I was a student, I along with my friends came to Chennai to celebrate Durga Puja. I met the secretary, who directed me to meet the in-charge of the ladies group. I met the lady, Mrs Banerjee along with Dipa. Mrs Banerjee she told me already she had a paying guest, who will vacate soon and then only she can accommodate Dipa. She also gave the address of a ladies hostel, which we visited, but it was bit far, so it was kept in reserve. I located the warden of Lord Ramakrishna, Sarda ladies hostel, which was strategically located in T. Nagar and the most safest destination for unmarried woman, but the only condition is that the candidate should have some connection with Ramkrishna mission activities. I gave a brief account of our association with Port Blair Rama Krishna Centre and my sister's three years

intimate involvement with R. K. Centre, Kolkata the lady was pleased and convinced with my briefings and ultimately agreed to provide accommodation to Dipa. The R. K. Centre, T.Nagar was operating from the heart of the city and Dipa's office i.e., CTS was a stone's throw distance. Though it had strict discipline and administration which was good for the unmarried young girls, we accepted it as it was a dream come true. The dishes were all vegetarian. Next day we went to the close-by market and bought all personal belongings for Dipa, entered the premises and I was waiting in the garden outside. After a couple of minutes Dipa returned and clarified that it was good, neat and clean, but you have to sit on the floor and take your food and wash your own utensils. I went back to my hotel that evening leaving behind Dipa in the hostel. I thanked God for finding a good and safe accommodation for her.

Next day my train was there from Madras Central at 10 p.m., met Dipa the next day evening, gave her some cash for emergencies and asked her to be very careful in the city and not to make too many friends as we are far off from Madras. She should also take care of her health and advised her to take milk and fruit juice regularly. I came back to my hotel, packed my luggage, and left for Madras Central Station, took dinner at the railway catering hall and waited for the train to arrive. At 10 pm, the train left the station. I was so tired, that immediately I moved on to the top of three tier sleeper and slept. Next Day and night, I was in the train and the next day early morning de-boarded at Kharagpur railway station took a rickshaw and reached home early in the morning. During the next available school break for Roopa's school, we decided to go to Chennai so that Lucky could meet Dipa see for herself, where she was staying. For the next visit, we planned and took the train to Chennai. Meanwhile Dipa regularly contacted us over the phone and told her about her company friends and R. K. Mission hostel life. We three reached Chennai, Dipa was at the station and took us all to a hotel in the heart of the city. Next day we went to her hostel. Dipa's Mom was allowed inside the hostel, she returned and told her that all the inmates had to sleep on floor and decided to contact and visit Mrs. Banerjee's residence for paying guest so that she could get Bengali dishes and also a better place to stay. Mrs. Banerjee was too glad to accept her as a paying guest. Dipa shifted from R. K. Mission ladies' hostel to Mrs. Banerjee's residence and continued, though it was a bit far from her office on Mount Road. Immediately after our return to Kharagpur, her mother started looking for a proper groom, to fix her marriage. She used to scan papers and write letters among many eligible bachelors, she located one match, a graduate engineer from IIT-Bombay whose father was in service in Bokaro, Bihar, showed interest inter-alia. After some correspondence we shortlisted three grooms for Dipa, as she had to come from Chennai taking leave. We coordinated in such a way that all three prospective grooms would be there in Kolkata, during a particular period. We booked IIT-KGP guest house at Salt Lake. Among the three prospective candidates we liked the IIT-Mumbai Boy and his father (Mr. Arun Kumar Sinha and Mrs. Purnima Sinha) as well their family. Dipa also had a chat with her would-be husband Bhaskar. While returning to IIT-KGP, we visited their house at Chetla(in Kolkata) to meet their relatives. The deal was almost finalized as both the parties agreed to tie the knot as early as possible. The earliest dates were scanned, and it was found that in December2003 there were few dates for marriage. At first, we thought of organizing it at IIT-KGP, but later had to change it as Mr. Sinha insisted that the marriage be held in Kolkata only. Organizing an event of this nature, away from home

Kharagpur, posed some logistic challenge, as all my resources were Kharagpur based, and organizing it at Barasat was a difficult task.

Since I had my own house in Barasat and my mother was staying there, and all my relatives are in Kolkata, inviting guests and friends was easy. The marriage was fixed on 9th December 2003. Dipa in the meantime requested her boss to consider her transfer to Poona as my would be son-in-law was employed with Geometric Software, Pune, a unit of Godrej Company. Her request was considered, and she was transferred to Pune. My son-in-law, Bhaskar arranged for her a P.G. accommodation in Pune.

I took leave for Dipa's wedding, my boss and Registrar was a strict officer and at the same time a reasonable and a considered officer too. My nephew's (Topu) marriage also took place in the same building named 'APSARA', which was strategically located in Barasat. The marriage went smoothly and after attending traditional Bow Bhat, (reception) we proceeded to KGP. A big responsibility was off loaded from our shoulder. Gradually Rupa was moving up in her school classes and we needed to pay attention to her.

After Dipa's marriage we all visited Pune, when they were in rented accommodation. We had gone to Goa on LTC and from there we went to Pune. After about two weeks of stay we returned to IIT-KGP. By then Dipa had already booked her new flat in a new complex which was under construction. Now our focus was on Rupa's academics. We were carefully monitoring her progress, especially screening her answer scripts in science and math.

In the year 2006, Rupa reached class X and was getting ready for her Board Exam for class 10.

After around two months the results were declared and she got 90 % marks, slightly below our expectation. Anyway, next was to get her admitted in Class XI of IIT-KGP, Kendriya Vidyalaya, which was in the campus. Depending upon marks obtained and availability of seats, Rupa got her admission, and we were relieved.

As time passed on, she moved from class 11 to class 12. By January 2008 her exam schedule was declared and her exam center was declared as K.V. Kalai Kunda, air force base Midnapore Dist. The school had arranged for buses. During her exam, my mother suffered a stroke and lost her speech. My brother-in-law and sister could do only what was possible, but then she lost her speech. I immediately went to Barasat to see her, but when I met her, she recognized me but was unable to talk. We called a local doctor, who said it was difficult to regain her speech. A maid was kept to feed her, bathe her but unfortunately she was confined to bed.

This was the saddest part of my life. As I came and narrated the story to lucky, I could not control my emotions, and broke down. Though at that point of time I had money, unlike during my father's illness (when I did not have sufficient money to treat him) but in the case of my mother, I was not there in Kolkata and I believe my brother-in-law could not provide the urgent medical aid, that was required in such cases. She survived for two weeks roughly, when I visited twice. For the duration, I was in Barasat I was by her bedside, when she was fed liquid diet and used to stare at me helplessly. I never felt so helpless during my life, it was so pathetic, a scene to watch. In the evening I returned to KGP in a pensive mood.

With in next three days, one morning, the news came from Barasat on 16th February 2008, that my mother had breathed her last. Hearing the news, I left KGP, along with Bishno (my close friend in KGP) and both of us were there in Barasat around 2pm. My elder cousin brothers from Barrackpore, other young boys from Barasat, joined and we left for the last and eternal journey of my mother to Barrackpore Crematorium, and with this memorable journey along with my mother's coffin, came an end of our affectionate bonding of fifty-seven years. I thanked God, Alas! "Ma Kali" was kind to hear my appeal and took her away and in a way relieved me from the sight of seeing her helplessly. I thanked God from the core of my heart.

Rupa's final exam despite (this family crisis) went off smoothly. I joined my office and gradually settled down, trying to mentally cope with this permanent loss. On one summer morning, while on a session of morning walk, I happened to meet one physics professor Dr. Sharma, who informed that my daughter (Rupa) had topped her Class XII, CBSE exam from IIT-KGP Kendriya Vidyalaya. When I asked him how did you come to know about it? He said "I saw it in the Dainik Jagran" a Hindi newspaper. Then I asked him, "can I get a copy?". He asked me to come to his residence. I collected the copy and came home running and then showed it to Rupa and Lucky. For a moment we just couldn't believe it. It was a joyous moment for us. The news spread like wildfire. Later Rupa received a trophy on the annual day of her school from the first lady of the IIT-KGP, campus.

Next came the Joint exams for admission to IIT's, NIT's, WBJEE, as well as private colleges like Vellore Institute of technology (VIT), Kalinga Institute of Technology (KIT) as well as Joint Entrance of Maharashtra state, were approaching fast.

Rupa continued her coaching. She appeared for IIT-JEE and AIEEE for admission to NIT's. The results were declared, and she could not clear IIT-JEE, nor WBJEE. Though she appeared for VIT joint entrance, but she could not clear VIT, but she cleared the KIIT joint entrance exam and got good ranking. We decided to accept the KIIT invitation and proceeded to Bhubaneswar to attend the admission and counseling programme.

I wanted her to accept the Electronics and Telecommunication branch, whereas Dipa wanted her to join Comp. Science. Engg stream. She had both options. Ultimately, she accepted Comp. Science and Engg branch. Her admission was confirmed and she paid the fees and got all her books, stationary, blazer as well as a Laptop.

After she moved into the hostel, Lucky saw her room and was satisfied. The next day we boarded the return Dhauli Express and came to Kharagpur. It was the year 2008. In the month of January 2008, we learnt that Dipa was expecting a baby. In the month of August 2008 (on 20th August) Doyel, my granddaughter, was born. It was a happy and momentous day for us. Lucky was already there in Pune. I was staying alone in IIT-KGP. As time flew my date of retirement was approaching fast and knocking at my door. When I take account of my past seventeen years of professional career, I feel satisfied that I have performed fairly well and earned respect from all quarters of IIT-KGP.

PART FOUR

2011 to 2021

...

My date of retirement was approaching fast. My date of retirement was 31st May 2011. Rupa started moving from first year to second year and from second year to third year and from third to fourth year. My date of retirement ultimately started knocking at my door. In the year 2011, on 31st may I laid down my office as Dy. Registrar (Estate Office) after almost 17 years of unblemished service.

During my tenure with IIT-KGP, I was given charge of almost all major departments excepting finance and accounts. The Major departments were a) Academics b) Administration c) Purchase d) Hall/Hostel management Centre e) Vinod Gupta School Of Management e) School of Intellectual property Law and Lastly f) Estate Office.

The estate office arranged a farewell and after the farewell, my professor in charge took me to the Director. Director thanked me for my services to IIT-KGP and offered me a memento. I met all the Deans in the Dean complex, and lastly spent a quality time with the Registrar and Dy Director who were my administrative and functional heads.

I served this famous institute with full dignity and honour and earned accolades from all the stakeholders, viz, students, teachers and administrative staff. The best part of my life was spent in IIT-Kharagpur and the **most precious part of it was it's beautiful library**. While in service I never craved for any position, nor did I flinch when any responsibility was thrusted on me. I took everything very graciously. While in service I was selected for the post(honorary) of Secretary, Institution of Engineers(I)[IIE] for the Kharagpur chapter as well as President of the Officers Association Of IIT-KGP. During my tenure as secretary at IIE I took the initiative to attract students (AMIE, Section A) from Midnapore district and arranged for their coaching classes with the help of Professors from IIT-KGP. Even I took Classes for Maths (only Calculus, both Differential and Integral) which was my pet topic in Maths. In all to sum up, I fully enjoyed my service of 17 years in IIT-KGP.

Immediately after my retirement I started applying to all private colleges. Suddenly and much to my surprise in the month of June 2011, I received a call from College of Engineering and Management Kolaghat (CEMK). Once the accommodation and other formalities were completed and finalized, we decided to move out of KGP.

Shifting from IIT-KGP to CEMK was a big setback for Lucky as the place was a desolate place as compared IIT-Campus. Besides, my office hours were too long as I had many challenges to set right the administrative set up. In the year 2012, Rupa graduated from KIIT University and I attended the convocation ceremony while Rupa was in Bangalore and working for Accenture. For three years I continued with CEMK.

In the year 2013, there was terrible unrest in the college and the college had to be closed down *sine die*, as one student committed suicide. In the same year, in the month of July, we had to go to Pune as Dipa was expecting her second Baby. On 1st July 2013, my second grandson **Dron** was born in Pune. We were there for about two weeks and after Dipa was released from the hospital we returned from Pune. In the year 2014, we decided to quit the Kolaghat job and move to Bangalore as Rupa's health was deteriorating, since she was not used to south Indian food. In the month of July, I tendered my resignation and moved out of CEMK, Kolaghat and shifted to Bangalore with lock stock and barrel. Settling down in Bangalore was a tough job as we were new to the city. We moved into a rented apartment and Rupa joined us. With in three months she started gaining her weight. She attended her office as well as her 'TIMES' coaching classes for Management entrance exam. As Bangalore was not liked by Lucky being far off from Kolkata her native place, she was feeling very lonely. Meanwhile Bhaskar and Dipa took her to Pune for a change . I and Rupa stayed and I used to cook and attend my school, (Gear International School,Bengaluru) where I used to take physics class for class 9 students of IGCSE Board-O-level.

Meanwhile lucky returned from Pune. Luckily, we could fix Rupa's groom, through newspaper, as also through Bharat Matrimony. We got three prospective grooms, among which we chose one whose parents were settled in north Kolkata and the groom did his graduation in engineering from JIS Group of Colleges. Currently he is employed with Vodafone and was posted in Mumbai. The groom named Indraneil Ghosh and his cousin brother Arnab who was then in Bengaluru, visited our place in Bengaluru. The conversation was cordial. After they went back, we got confirmation from groom's father Ghosh Babu (from Kolkata), that they were interested in the deal. But my school termin Bangaluru was to end on 19th April 2015.Hence I had to wait. As usual the final exam ended, PTM(Parent Teachers Meet) was held, and I was relieved, after a farewell.

Meanwhile based upon a request from Rupa, her employer Accenture transferred her from Bengaluru to Mumbai, Vikhroli office. Rupa started staying in P.G. accommodation in Mumbai. We fixed a Packer and mover and booked our household goods and we left Bengaluru by flight. For seven days in Kolkata, we managed our food and with partial furniture, which were there in Garia. After a week our furniture and car arrived, and we slowly settled down. In the month of May 2015, Shri Ghosh Babu insisted that the marriage registration be finalized and we agreed to it Accordingly the marriage was registered at Belghoria(In North Kolkata). The traditional marriage day was fixed on 26th Nov'2015. As soon we settled down in Garia and the registration was finalized, we started gearing up for the real showdown fixed on 26th Nov 2015.Since there were no one along with us we had to arrange for this ceremony all alone right from dresses ornaments, caterer, decorator, marriage Hall etc. Luckily near Garia(In South Kolkata) and on Patuli Road we got a spacious marriage hall on the ground floor itself. Dipa and Bhaskar came just in time and helped us a lot. The wedding went smoothly and almost all the guests who were invited attended the marriage.

On our part, as parents we heaved a sigh of relief as our responsibility as parents came to an end. From the day Both Dipa and Rupa were born, we were under constant pressure as to whether, they would be able to settle in life.

By the grace of God, hard work and honest dealings throughout my life and Lucky's wholehearted and dedicated service, I think we could achieve this. I owe much to this success as blessings from my parents, so also to Lucky who had steered through my turbulent life with awesome success. I thanked God that both my daughters had lived up to our expectations. Throughout their school, college life and other associations, we did not receive a single complaint from the society around us regarding their character or from their teachers during their entire academic journey. Few parents are lucky to be rewarded with this gift.

After Rupa got settled in Mumbai, we visited Mumbai twice. We were greatly satisfied by the hospitality of her In-Laws and her husband Indraneil. He is also a foody person, smart and easy-going and can be friendly with anyone very easily.

In the year 2016, precisely 27th November, Rupa gave birth to a baby boy. It was a joyous moment for all of us. We were in Mumbai, but at the same time her in Laws also arrived in Mumbai. Anyway after a few months Rupa along with her baby came to Garia. During their stay, Dipa and Bhaskar along with Doyel and Dron also came to Garia. It was a family get together with a lot of fun. Especially Doyel and Dron enjoyed with Ishaan a lot. Time flies and after a few days they left for Mumbai.

Though our stay in Garia had all the plus points but the location of the house, its surroundings and especially our apartment residents, their attitude was not very welcoming. I on my part wanted to bring in some discipline regarding financial transactions in the society, but I failed.

Thus, in consultations with Dipa we decided to look for a gated community apartment, commensurate with our social standing, mental thinking, likes and dislikes. While we were in Kharagpur Dipa had booked a flat in Uniworld City (UWC), in Rajarhat New town, a large gated complex developed by M/s Unitech, a fairly reputed developer from Delhi. For quite some time we visited the complex to see the progress of the construction and in fact we liked it. The final deal for a two bed roomed flat in Uniworld City at Rajarhat Newtown was struck and in October 2017, immediately after puja we shifted. Bhaskar came to help us in shifting from Garia to UWC.

At UWC, we re-discovered our real home, a pleasant calm and ecofriendly atmosphere far from the madding crowd and the din and bustle of city life. Meanwhile Bhaskar changed his company and moved from Geometric Software Pune, to Schnieder Electric, Hyderabad. Rupa also acquired new flat in the smart city of PALAVA, in Dombivli East. After a week's stay in Mumbai on 29th February 2020, we took a flight and landed in Hyderabad. By then, the ghost pandemic Covid 19 also landed in Kerala. The news that pandemic Covid 19 had already started infecting the world started pouring in like wildfire. On 23rd March, while we were in Hyderabad along with Dipa the first ill-fated Lock down was declared and we were stranded in Hyderabad, Aparna Sarovar complex.

Every one of us is aware how difficult was our life during this lock down. From March 2020 till July 2020, we were in Hyderabad. During this period, Dipa arranged for my cataract operation in L.V. Prasad Eye Hospital, one of the best hospitals in the country. The operation went smoothly. After the operation and clearance by the doctor we decided to move out of Hyderabad. After landing in Kolkata on 22nd July 2020 and initial settling down, I started writing down my memoir and today is 30th July 2021 almost after a year the memoir is now ready for proof reading and editing. Without my cataract operation in Hyderabad, writing this memoir would have been impossible. Dipa's contribution and encouragement has been immense in writing this memoir.

While I am advancing in my age, reminiscent of the past continues to haunt me and a reflection of the past memories, both sweet and sour are to be penned down.

My regrets

- During my childhood days in Port Blair, When I was very young around 5 years old, Naval ships from Indian navy as well as from British Navy used to visit Port Blair and school children were taken around these ships as a part of school excursion. I paid my first visit to INS MYSORE. It was in the year 1955. The next visit was paid to a British Royal Navy Ship. The white dress, the smart officers, the small speed boats driven by the Coxswain all delighted my dream of joining the navy. Added to it, our house was on the top of a hill, barely 500m away from the open sea from where I could see the Naval ships anchored, with the flying colors of their national flags. All these events terribly aroused my interest and my dream to join the Indian Navy. I decided to join Indian Navy immediately after my engineering graduation. Till the second year of my engineering course, I was not aware that wearing glasses would debar me from joining any defense services. In the year 1969, I went for correction of my glasses when I asked the doctor, whether I could join the navy, but the doctor quietly answered in a negative way. I was very depressed, and my dream turned out to be a dream only.

- My second regret is despite my good health and willingness to work hard with honesty, I missed two golden opportunities in NDDB, since I joined the Company in 1978. The first one was in 1980, due to my family's economic condition the second was one was 1985 when the Director wanted me take up construction of a milk spray drying plant under the supervision of a FAO consultant. Thus I fell back on my professional career and could not make up the loss till my retirement.

My Regards

My sincere regards to a few people, especially those teachers, who were instrumental in shaping my life (other than my parents and the environment in which I grew up). These are appended below with a very short note and in ascending order in terms of their teaching timeline.

- **Teachers of Modern Preparatory School (Cambridge system of Education), Port Blair, Andaman and Nicobar Islands.**

o Mrs. Horner, Mrs. Wiggins and Mrs. Williams our British teachers from Nursery to Kinder- Garden-I&II.

o Mrs. V. K. Srinivasan, B.A from Madras University, who taught us English and Mrs. Bani Chakraborty, B.A. from Calcutta University, who taught us History and Geography, in the Senior KG

o Mrs. Smriti Kana Sanyal, our Head Mistress and a graduate from Calcutta University and trained in U.K. in Cambridge system of Curricula. These teachers taught us (besides the normal school curricula, discipline and social etiquette),love respect and duty towards society and fellow classmates, who were from varied countries like Burma, Japan, China British, including Anglo-Indians etc.

- **Secondary School teachers Of Govt,Higher Secondary Multipurpose School ,Port Blair(From 1963-68)**

o Shri Mansha Ram Gupta, Teacher for Maths and Chemistry. A very sincere and dedicated teacher, to whom I pay my highest regards.

o Our Principal late Brojendra Lal Shah, who taught us Physics.

o Our English teacher Khan Sir, a tall fair complexioned hand some personality from Delhi Public school. I wonder how affectionate one could be with the students. He was a bachelor. He narrated us so nicely about as to how he continued to remain a bachelor. Mr. Khan said "My marriage train came to the station and waited for me, I was running to board the train, before I could board the train, the train started gushing and moved on, and I was helplessly staring at the train and cursing my fate. I missed my marriage train. In short, this is my marriage story. Students heard the story of Khan Sir, with rapt silence. I wonder how nicely he narrated his story??

- **Teachers Of Annamalai University, Dept of Engineering.(From 1968-1973)**

o Prof D Rama Ratnam, MSc; who taught us Calculus in the first year. A masterpiece teacher who taught us in a beautiful and enriching manner a subject like Calculus.

o Prof V R Muthhuverrapan, an M.S. from Cornell University, USA who instilled in me confidence of studying and understanding Thermodynamics, considered as a highly conceptual subject in Mechanical Engineering. He helped me to clear the subject, much to the surprise of even the very best students of my class.

My last respect

It is said in Lord Budha's teachings that "It would be impossible for a son to pay his parents for their gracious kindness, even if he could carry his father on his right shoulder and his mother on his left for one hundred long years". Further Budha's blessing abides in the home where parents are held in respect and esteem. Whatever I am today, much of it, I owe to my parents, as also to my sister Rekha, who supported me financially for five years during my engineering course,in Annamalai University, while serving as a teacher in Rabindra Bangla Vidyalaya, a Bengali medium Govt school in Port Blair.

Epilogue

...

At seventy-one, I do think of death, but I don't lose sleep over it. I think of those gone; keep wondering where they have gone? Where will they be? I don't know the answers-where you go and what happens next. I do not know where I will be in another two to three years. What I fear is the day when I am physically incapacitated because of old age. I don't want to be an extra burden on my wife as well my daughter Dipa. But it is not my choice. I shall be led by my destiny. Above all, when the time comes to go, one should go like a man, without any regret or grievance against any one, whether alive or dead. Though I am physically and mentally fit, but I know I don't have much time left. I am coming to terms with death, preparing myself as each day passes by. To the best of my ability, I have tried to fulfill my obligations to my family and to society at large. At the far end of my journey, I realized that nothing in the world can strictly be called as mine. Whatever has come to me, is a gift of God and of my past doings. Some of it must be shared with others who are in dire need, keeping aside some money for your own emergency use.

I am happy that that I have been able to complete my memoir, during this pandemic and live up to the expectations and assurances given to my daughters Jayita, Ankita and my granddaughter, Doyel while we were in Hyderabad.

A note of condolence in memory of my sister Rekha and my brother-in-law Dr. Barid Kanti Ray, both of whom I lost during this pandemic. My only sister Rekha nick name named 'Manu' was elder to me by around four years and was born on an auspicious day of Christmas on 25th December 1946 in Port Blair, when Britishers were still present in large numbers. Naturally we used to religiously celebrate her birthday each year, in whatever manner we could as a humble and frugal family. After graduation from Calcutta University in 1966 she served as a teacher in Rabindra Bangla Vidyalaya school till 1973.

After reading, the readers will be able to gauge the personality of the person who was an island of sensibility, surrounded by the cool sense of his wife, children and friends.

--END--

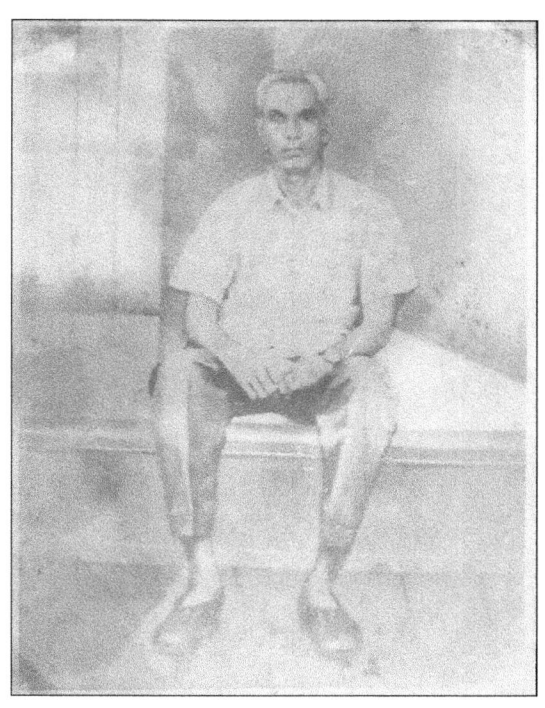

Father Late Sushil Kumar Basu Roy Chowdhury'

Mother Late Sudharani Basu Roy Chowdhury

With school friends in 1968.

With sister Rekha .

Engieering College Passout 1973

With wife Maya.

www.ingramcontent.com/pod-product-compliance
Lightning Source LLC
LaVergne TN
LVHW061553070526
838199LV00077B/7035